PLAYING POKER AGAINST THE MOB

The Joe Cammarano Story

PART 1

JEFF LISANDRO

Playing Poker Against the Mob: The Joe Cammarano Story

Copyright © 2023 by Jeff Lisandro.

PB: ISBN: 978-1-63812-585-3
Ebook ISBN: 978-1-63812-584-6

All rights reserved. No part in this book may be produced and transmitted in any form or by any means, electronic, or mechanical, including photocopying, recording, or by any information storage and retrieval system, without permission in writing from the copyright owner.

The views expressed in this work are solely those of the author and do not necessarily reflect the views of the publisher hereby disclaims any responsibility for them.
Published by Pen Culture Solutions 01/19/2023

Pen Culture Solutions
1-888-727-7204 (USA)
1-800-950-458 (Australia)
support@penculturesolutions.com

Table of Contents

Preface 5

Poker in the Cross 7
Perth 9
Dealing in Sydney 11
The Italian Job 13
Money Matters 15
A Game of Skill 18
Trouble Brewing 23
Fight Night 26
Forced Out 31
The Aussie Mob 35
Chinese Gang Bang 39

The Bookie 47
My First Million 49
The Player 55
Party Time 57
The High Life 61
Appearance is Everything 68
The Sauna 70
SP Bookmaker 73
Bookie's Runner 76

Toss the Coins. 82
I Leave the Underworld 87

Russia. 89
Flight to Russia 91
The Russian Office 95
A Luxury Apartment 98
The Penta Hotel .102
Getting My Share 104
Gabriella's Casino 109
A Georgian Meal 112
A Hot Dog in Red Square 116
Poker at the Royal 118
Real Room Service 120
I Can Do This on My Own 123
Poker Interrupted 126
The Novy Arbat 128
Security at Gabriella's 131
Disappearing Businessmen 134
Otari's Funeral. 137
My New Apartment 138
Our Casino Opens 141
Exit Plan 143
Airport Escape .146
Three Capitals .147
Coming Soon: Part Two 151
Joe Cammarano Will Return 152

Preface

This is the first of three books of a story by Australia's most successful poker player, Jeff Lisandro. It is a work of fiction, based on Jeff's own experiences. Names have been changed. Conversations have been re-imagined. Some events have been combined, and some have been fictionalised. In movie terms, *Playing Poker Against the Mob* is "Based on the incredible story of Jeff Lisandro."

Jeff is a natural storyteller, both in person and in print. He has a phenomenal memory and remembers the events of the 1980s and 1990s as though they happened last week. Jeff has had nine lives, both through leading an event-filled life, and by cheating death. He has been involved in illegal casinos in Sydney's Kings Cross and surrounding suburbs in the 1980s. You may think that this involved standing a polite distance from the poker table and dealing with player disputes, like a modern-day poker supervisor… It was a lot rougher than that. Jeff's trip to Moscow to set up a casino was even more dangerous.

POKER IN THE CROSS

Perth

This is my story of how a boy from Perth found himself in Moscow at the beginning of 1993. At the age of sixteen years old, I had to leave school and earn my own money, even though I was a brilliant student. Due to family problems, I couldn't continue my studies. I started off as a junior clerk in the Perth Transport Department, five days a week. I had a second job over the weekends in a restaurant; as a waiter, dishwasher and assistant cook. I absorbed everything I was exposed to, always thinking how these things could assist me in my later life.

Two or three times a week, I organized poker games. Before long I gave up on my other jobs and concentrated on running and playing in the poker nights. The money I made doing this was way more than I made doing the traditional jobs.

My father had worked in the mining industry for over 30 years, earning a lot of money only to lose it gambling and never having much to show for his hard work. As I neared my seventeenth birthday, Dad had an idea. He begged me to stop gambling and work with him instead, in pipeline construction and exploration drilling.

"In my whole lifetime, I've never met anyone who has made money gambling."

"Dad, you're a terrible gambler" I replied. "I, on the other hand, am a brilliant gambler. But I will need a bankroll to make serious money."

He then offered me a highly paid job to be his assistant in the Outback. The pay was roughly five times the average wage, excellent money for a seventeen-year-old. I travelled all through Western Australia for a year, tens of thousands of miles through some of the most remote parts of Australia: Kalgoorlie to Kununurra. It was hard work with long hours, and very lonely. Dad and I sometimes met co-workers, prospectors and geologists to analyse the samples we'd drilled. The rest of the time it was just the two of us.

As Christmas 1983 approached, I was now eighteen years old. Dad and I had two weeks off. We returned to Perth for some well-earned holidays. A decision was approaching. I now had $30,000 in the bank, and an average house was $50,000 in those days. Dad told me, "If you work with me another two years, you'll have enough to buy two houses."

But this mining work wasn't for me. I felt I could do better on the poker tables and enjoy myself more. I had discovered the attractions of women and having a good time. There was none of that on a distant mining trip. Right after New Year, Dad said, "Four more days and it's back to work for us." I didn't know what to say. As much as I'd enjoyed the year working with Dad, the isolation was unbearable. The following day I told him "I'm not going with you, Dad. I have my own plans. I'm going to Sydney. I hear there are poker games there every night. Five to ten different places, underground casinos, with blackjack too."

Dad was very upset. He enjoyed my company and was worried about me on the other side of the continent in this gangster-type environment. He knew I could handle myself and had seen me fight guys twice my size. But the newspapers had stories about gang wars raging in Sydney. Every week it seemed someone was killed. He begged me not to go, but my decision was final.

Dealing in Sydney

I arrived in Sydney two days later. I met up with a Chinese guy who ran a poker game in Double Bay. I knew him and some other Chinese men from Perth, where they'd taught me to deal the card games they played. Some of their games weren't traditional poker games, where players fight to win a pot, but were still gambling games using cards.

The Chinese knew I was new to Sydney and needed a job, so they only paid me half of what they paid their other dealers. Their clubs had many players and were making heaps of money in rake. The gangsters who owned the clubs didn't see how lucrative the business was. Between all these Chinese, they developed a society – a Mob. They supported each other and pushed out the Australians and the Europeans. They had Double Bay to themselves. I was just an eighteen-year-old with limited finances, who they could pay at half-wages, and I didn't look like a threat to them.

After a few months they become nasty towards me. They wanted me to train young Chinese boys to deal. I could see that I was training my replacements, but agreed and trained the new dealers.

The Chinese were humble and friendly around Westerners, smiling and looking weak. But behind our backs they were taking every dollar they could get their hands on. They were also involved in the illegal drug trade, and didn't like me observing their conversations. They had unconditional loyalty to each other, and preferred employing their fellow Chinese wherever possible, forcing out workers like me.

A few weeks after the young Chinese dealers were on board, I was told "Fuck off and go back to Perth. You don't work here anymore." That came as no surprise. I'd been expecting it and it was time to move on.

Not back to Perth though. I'd saved some money and I'd seen how the Chinese operated their casinos. They had forty to fifty members, and four clubs in the best locations. There were plenty of other underground casinos, probably eight or so. I could apply what I'd seen in the Chinese rooms and start some poker elsewhere.

The Italian Job

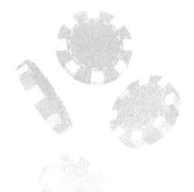

I approached an Italian man who ran a small casino in Kings Cross. I told him that I could start a poker game on his premises. I'd manage the staff, dealers, waitresses, security and credit to the customers. He'd handle the standover men. I proposed a 75/25 split of the poker money with him. I'd play in the games with my own money, keeping my winnings and liable for all my losses.

To run a good poker game, I had to be prepared and capable of playing in the game myself. If five players were in the club and a sixth player was needed to get the game running, I had to be that sixth player. If the game wasn't running, I wasn't making money.

I was still only eighteen years old, and I seemed like an easy target for the gangsters and rival operators. However, I knew what I was up against and I was fit for the challenge. The first few nights went OK with takings of $1,500 and $1,700. I was up a few hundred on my own poker play. My Italian partner was happy. On the fourth night, a local gangster started playing. He was not the kind of customer I wanted but he had money and wasn't that good of a player. After a few hours he was down $3,000 and I'd won most of it. He turned to me and asked if he could borrow a thousand dollars. I'd been warned that this guy didn't repay his credit. I had to make a quick decision on how to handle this situation.

Instead of a yes or no, I found a third way: "I'm sorry, this is our first week, we're just getting started and the business can't give credit yet." He didn't like this answer and steam was coming out of his ears. "But I can give you $500 to play in a different establishment. I know who you are, and people respect you." That cooled him down. I reached into my own pocket and gave him the five hundred. "Pay me back when you're comfortable., anytime you want," I added. He took the money, thanked me, smiled, and left the room. The poker game continued in his absence and it was a great night. I made $2,500 profit and word was getting around that we had a good game going here.

Business picked up even more the next week, we had games running every night. Some Asians started coming into the casino. A few were players, but most were rival operators, unhappy that they were losing customers and business to us. They thought I was out of my depth and we'd either go broke or run into the wrong customer. Most customer issues can't be fixed with $500 gifts. Security was a constant concern for the casinos.

Money Matters

My next problem was cash. I had to much of it and I needed a way to store it safely. Any big bank deposit over the counter would attract suspicion and that was the only way you could do banking in those days. Luckily, Australia had just introduced hundred-dollar notes and they were proving very popular in the casinos. If all my cash was in fifties, it would have taken up twice the space. I had a huge sum of $60,000. I needed about $15,000 of that on hand for loans to customers and my own poker play. I could carry a few thousand safely enough, but I needed a safe way of storing forty thousand dollars. I had to be careful not to have too much cash on me at any one time.

I was safe enough inside the club, but the outside was another story. I approached my Italian partner and asked him to keep $40,000 of my money in his safe. His 25% share had netted him $50,000 without extra work or risk to him, and I'd taken his casino to a higher level. What I didn't see at the time was his envy of the money I was making. He made the right noises every time I saw him, smiling and telling me what a good job I was doing and how happy he was that his casino was so busy. While he was doing a great out of our deal, he never saw our arrangement as a partnership, and he wasn't happy that an upstart young kid was making so much money himself.

I managed over time to deposit $30,000 into Dad's account but for a few months later, I needed some of that forty thousand dollars back from my boss. I asked him for it.

"What?" he cried.

"I need some of that forty thousand I left you. I'm short on cash right now and I need money to run the game tonight."

He was angry, and so was I. It was my money and I needed it. He went into his office and came back with just four thousand dollars and said "That's all I have."

He'd screwed me. I discussed the situation with the security doorman with whom I was friendly. I'd tipped him $20 now and then for his good work. He told me that the boss was upset at all the easy money that young Joe was making and intended to run the game himself.

"Why would he be jealous? He's making more than me!" I said.

The roulette and blackjack side of the casino was making The Italian much more than what I made on poker. Tough. The other $36,000, whether it was still in the safe or The Italian had already spent it, was no longer mine. I'd banked $40,000 with The Italian and got one-tenth of it back, just three months later. Don't ever complain to me about your bank's account-keeping fees.

The gangsters started re-appearing at the casino and they wanted me to give them money. I went home and decided I couldn't continue in this situation. I wasn't going to tell the boss about the money I'd sent to Dad. I'd pretend to be broke and to have lost my money on horserace betting (I obviously hadn't lost big in my poker games). You only have enemies in this business when you still have money. If you're broke, you're powerless, pitied and ignored.

So, I came in the next night and told the boss I had no more money. He said see you later, just leave and never tell anyone about the money in the safe. So, I left, he was happy. He thought I was flat broke and that he could run the game himself without me. it was another lesson for me to absorb. Trust no-one in this business.

A Game of Skill

Taking stock, I was alive, with $30,000 safely in Dad's account and a year's experience in dealing games, playing games, and running games. I went back to Perth to reunite with my family and my money. I couldn't have picked a better time to be away from Sydney. Four weeks after I returned to Perth, the Sydney casinos were shut down.

After another month relaxing in Perth, I returned to Sydney to see with my own eyes what was really going on. The casinos were indeed closed but were about to re-open under restrictive new laws. These laws would actually help poker at the expense of blackjack, roulette, baccarat and two-up.

The new laws said that only eight people could be playing at a time and they had to be playing games of skill, not games of chance. Poker was a game of skill under their definition (no argument from me). Players in a crowded casino or players of games of chance risked fines of $1,000 each.

I went looking for new premises in which I could run a poker game. I was told of a Chinese guy, Mr. Choong, who had an interest in a closed-up casino that could be re-opened. I went to speak with him.

Mr. Choong told me he had a great location, in the centre of the Cross, but his rent was $5,000 a month. I knew the place and it was ideal. I told him that I could give him $10,000 a month and take over the room for him. I added that I didn't want him coming into the place and I didn't need him interfering with my set-up. It would be hard for his place to run other games under the new laws, just let me a run a poker game and that's $10,000 a month for him; double what his rent was. He told me that I couldn't make so much money just from a poker game and that he needed two months up-front and $10,000 per month on the first of every month.

I realised that I needed more capital. My plan was good, but I needed $40,000: $20,000 for those two months upfront, and another $20,000 to loan to customers and for my own playing.

I went outside, sat down on a bench, and thought about how I could get the seed money for the cardroom. I didn't have many options. As luck would have it, a Russian guy I knew saw me sitting there and sat down to talk to me. He once short-charged me $100 but I wasn't going to remind him of that now.

"Joe! Fancy seeing you out here!"

"Oh hey there Sergei. Nice to see you."

"It's such rotten luck that the casinos are all shut down. What are you going to do with yourself now?"

"Oh, I've got a brilliant idea. I can make $10,000 dollars a week."

"And just how will you do that?"

"I'm going to start a poker room, right in the middle of Kings Cross."

"Well, that's great, but nobody ever made ten thousand dollars a week by running a poker game." After expenses, existing poker games made about $3,000 a week.

"Well, I figure I can." I told him.

"Why do you think that?"

"Because I'm the best in this business."

"So do it then," he said.

"Yeah, well I'm a bit short of capital."

"OK well, tell me your business plan."

Sure. Let me tell you all my ideas, for free, so you can start up your own cardroom or get other people to do it for you. I'm pretty sick of my ideas being stolen and being forced out of my jobs and having others take over. "I can't trust you with my business plans."

"Well, you have to trust someone, Joes, and if I like your idea I might come up with your capital. How much are we talking about?"

"I need forty thousand. Can you come up with forty thousand?"

"It's a drop in the ocean." Forty thousand is a drop in the ocean and yet he stiffed me for a hundred that time.

"OK, I'll tell you the business plan. A twenty-four-hour cardroom. Not just weekends. Twenty-four-seven. Three shifts a day, eight-hour shifts. We'll take in between $1,000 and $2,000 each shift. That's five grand a day." When they were running, the existing Sydney casinos were overnight operations, open from 7 p.m. to 7 a.m. Weekends were all-day, all-night.

"Who wants to play poker on a weekday between 7 a.m. and 7 p.m.? People work, there won't be any players."

"You can only have eight players maximum anyway, some people play in the day and they'll have to play with us. We'll be the only game in town during those hours."

"Not for long you won't. If daytime gambling made sense, the other places would've done it before now. Surely they've thought about it too."

"The other people aren't businessmen, they're not that smart and they're not hard workers. Just do the Maths. $5,000 a day for 30 days is $150,000 a month. I control the whole thing, the rent is $10,000 per month, wages are $45,000 per month, $40,000 a month for bad loans, leaving me with $55,000 a month. I can do this, Sergei. I'm young, I'm strong, I've got incredible stamina."

"You've got incredible chutzpah if you ask me. So, your best-case scenario is $150,000 a month?"

"No, I think I can make more." I'm convinced of this myself and my conviction is starting to win him over.

"OK, if I came up with forty thousand, what security do you have?"

"None whatsoever."

"I was afraid of that. Can you pay $4,000 per week interest?"

Loan-shark rates. "That's a lot, but I can do it."

"So now you need to find some collateral."

Collateral? It's not my premises and I'll need the little money I have left if my house of cards falls over like a house of cards. "Look, I won't lie to you. I'm eighteen and half years old, I'm scared of no-one but if this fucks up, I can't pay you back. But as long as I'm operating, I promise you the $4,000 a week interest and then one thousand a week on-going, even after I pay you back the forty."

Sergei likes this, but he's still looking for some kind of guarantee that he'll get something back if the venture fails early. "Well, if you go broke, you pay me what you can."

"No, I can't do that. If I go broke, you get back nothing, game over, you lose your money just like I do."

"I have to think about it." He takes a few minutes but there's $40,000 coming my way. "I hope I don't regret this. It's a deal, Joe."

"Thanks. It's the best deal."

With the seed money secured, I went to Mr. Choong to say the cardroom was on. I'd start on the first of next month, just three days away. I gave him the $20,000 two-month deposit and told him that I was making the decisions. I was hiring the doorman, waitress and dealers. He could get his $10,000 on the first of each month. And I made my own business.

I started the first 24-hour a day poker game, as legal as a Sydney casino was possible to be. Sergei himself was the first costumer. A few small-time players came in and then the big fish, Katya. A wealthy Russian lady. She was a whale of the Sydney gambling scene.

After just four hours, there was a full table of eight players, with ten on the waiting list. I thanked everyone for coming and reminded them that we never close and the action is 24-hours here. Free coffee and drinks all day, and I'll buy everyone lunch at 2 p.m.

Lots of people came in looking for a job. We soon had an excellent staff complement for each of the three shifts. Our first takings were exceeding $5,000 a day by some margin. First $7,200. Then $8,000. Then $7,000. It was like we had a money printing machine. And people can never leave money printing machines alone.

Trouble Brewing

The money-printing machine coughed and spluttered on the fourth day. Mr. Choong came into the club and took me aside for a chat.

"Joe, we have a problem. Some gangsters came in asking of this place is still mine. They want protection money from us."

"I'll talk to them. I'll get it sorted out."

"No, Joe, it's too late for that. They are serious people. I told them it's my place, but you're renting it from me. We agreed that I'll give them $1 500 a week."

"You shouldn't have done that without asking me."

"No, I'll handle it. Just give me the money and I'll pass it on to them."

I wasn't happy with him making decisions by himself and I let him know that. But I also sensed that he wasn't grateful for my work in running the room. He'd estimated the money I was making and was no longer happy with his flat rate of $10,000 per month.

In the fourth week, before he had even got his second $10,000 monthly payment, Mr. Choong tried again. He came to me in tears. "What's wrong?" I asked him.

"Joe, I know we agreed on ten thousand a month but it's not fair! You're making fifty thousand a week."

"No, I'm not. Mr. Choong, if I make $500 a week, I have to pay you just the same, you told me that yourself. If I don't make the $10,000 on the first of each month, I'm out and I lose my $20,000 deposit. That's our deal."

"No, Joe. My partners have told me we have to change the deal."

"Partners? You never told me you had partners."

"Of course I have partners. Stan the Man, Graham Brown and Jimmy Heartless."

No way were those guys partners. This was a classic standover trick. Name dropping. Mr. Choong simply mentioned some well-known gangsters as his partners. Maybe Meyer Lansky was in on the action too.

"So what are you proposing?"

"We can do it this way: I'll hire the doormen, and the partners and I will make twenty percent." Mr. Choong would be lucky to have anything left for himself, after paying his gangster-legend partners and protection racketeers. "I'm sorry about this Joe. You know, I spent $200,000 renovating this place, and I need some chance of getting that investment back."

In fairness to Mr. Choong, his club was well fitted-out and a lot of money had been spent on it. And there were powerful gangsters running protection over the casinos. His claim for $1,500 a week sounded truthful. He wanted to hand over the money to the protection guys himself, keeping me in the background. He would have the prestige of running this successful poker club all to himself.

I told Mr. Choong I'd have his second $10,000 ready for him on schedule and I'd have a reply to his new twenty percent demand. I wanted some time to think about it. I sought out Sergei for his advice.

"Pay him his twenty percent, you'll still make plenty."

I thought about that. I also heard that a group of Malaysian Chinese were set to copy my set-up, with their own 24/7 cardroom down the road. I had no written contract and if Mr. Choong wanted to go it alone, he could simply force me out and take over. My decision was to stay. The money-printing machine chugged along, but Mr. Chong couldn't stop jamming the works.

Halfway into our second month, he came into the room and told all the waitresses that this was their last week and he got new people to replace them. The new waitresses were no better than the ones I hired. Mr. Choong was just showing off that he was the real boss around here.

I hired a junior partner, Robin, to handle the room in my resting hours. Robin was a Chinese friend of mine from Perth days and had a lot of gambling experience. He was forty-five years old and had known Mr. Choong for twenty years. Robin had managed a Mahjong Club years ago. Mr. Choong had been a regular there, sleeping in the corner, eating the free food, and trying to borrow money from costumers. Robin had kicked him out of the club. Mr. Choong didn't like someone who knew his past being part of my operation. He asked me not to hire Robin, but I told him I'd hire whoever I wanted as my junior partner, especially since Mr. Choong had now taken over the doormen, waitresses, and was getting a big percentage of the takings.

So, I kept Robin and he was popular, honest, and hard working. The Malaysian Chinese opened up their cardroom nearby, but they couldn't take our players.

Fight Night

Players would gamble at multiple clubs and some would play at a club while owing money to another club. We had a well-establishment rule that poker room owners wouldn't chase players when they were in other poker rooms.

I agreed with this rule but the punishment for breaking it was severe. My best costumer was an old Russian lady. She owed money to both me and one of the Chinese clubs. One day she was in my room playing and the Chinese operator from the club down the road comes right in and asks her to come outside and talk to him. Everyone could see it was about money owed. I was fuming. This was totally disrespectful to my establishment. After a few minutes she began crying, the game stopped, and people looked to me to intervene. As I got closer to the Chinese guy, I saw he had a gun pointed at the old Russian lady. I grabbed it off him, much to his surprise. He struggled to regain it, so I slapped him, picked him up and threw him outside on the street.

I tossed the gun aside and went back into the poker room. Everyone was laughing in relief, but the trouble wouldn't stay outside for long. Thirty minutes later I heard the door being smashed and people yelling. The Chinese guy had returned and this time he had friends; about twenty Chinese from the competing poker room. They had knives, num-chuks, meat cleavers and baseball bats. They invited me to come outside. This was serious. I walked up to the guy I'd ejected and told him he'd broken the rules by coming in to chase his debt, in my club, and pointing a gun at one of my players.

The supporting Chinese chatted among themselves. I sensed they were worried about the consequences of his actions. They hadn't heard my side of the story, they thought they were just revenging an unfair eviction. As their discussion continued, I told them I was going to call Mr. Choong and his partners to come in. Two or three of the angry Chinese could stay and help sort the situation out, the rest of them had to leave. The evictee said "Ok, well call him." I called him from the phone, in full view of everybody. All eyes were on me as I made the call.

Luckily, he was home and answered the call. I told him truthfully what had happened and that there were now twenty Chinese in the club with weapons. I needed him to come in and help defuse the situation. He was no help at all.

"I'm not coming in. You need to sort your own problems out," he said and hung up on me.

The unwanted Chinese guests hadn't heard the hang-up. I stayed on the phone and pretended the conversation was still going. After three more minutes, I ended this conversation and walked right up to the guys with the weapons. "Right, like I said before, three of you can stay and the rest of you are leaving now." I marched most of them off the premises. Our doorman, who had boasted he was a Vietnam veteran, was nowhere to be seen. He'd bolted as soon as the Chinese gang had arrived.

I returned to the three Chinese guys still in the club and offered them a drink. Mr. Choong would be here in 45 minutes, they were welcome to wait. They cooled down and I started up the poker game again. I returned to the Chinese and tried to reason with them.

"I shouldn't have hit you," I told the guy I'd evicted, "but I just reacted to the situation with the gun."

"When is Mr. Choong coming?" he asked.

"Pretty soon," I lied, "but if he doesn't arrive you are welcome to come back at midday."

He sensed I was lying about Mr. Choong coming in, but he wasn't angry anymore. He felt he'd accomplished his goal. He had saved face in front of the other Chinese after his public eviction. The three Chinese all left soon after, even saying goodbye to me.

I sensed that my days were numbered in this club. Because the business I'd set up was going so well, Mr. Choong wanted the money, the power, and the feeling of being in charge of it. He also wanted the glory of saying it was all his idea and I'd just been getting in his way. So, I decided to play it smart, be low-key, just jeep accumulating money, and stay out of people's way. Maybe in a few months, I'd have enough money saved that I could afford to rent my own premises.

By the end of the fourth month, things were getting unbearable. Mr. Choong was openly meeting other Chinese operators and it was becoming obvious that they were going to make him an offer to take over my side of the business.

The doorman, who now wouldn't look me in the eye, couldn't be counted on to protect me even inside the premiss. An ex-boxer with a drug problem, about 35 years old, began playing in my club. On the first night he asked me for $100 to get him home and I gave it to him, even though we didn't make that much from his play at the table. The next night he returned, high-fived the doorman and asked for $200 straight away. I told him, "No, not today."

He replied, "You fucker, if you don't give it to me, you'll have a problem when you go outside."

Things were getting tough. I was a one-man target, and I wasn't getting help from my employer or our useless doorman. I agreed to the boxer's offer of trouble. "As it happens, I am leaving now, so come outside and do your best." As I was walking out, the doorman laughed in my face. One of the players warned me not to take the boxer on. "Don't do it Joe; he's a pro fighter, he's had 23 fights, 20 wins, 15 by knockout." I wondered if someone was framing a betting market. Cammarano knocked out in the second round would be the shortest price.

I thanked the player for his warning, but I had to show these guys I was no pushover. The room emptied as everyone came to watch the fight. I sized up my opponent. His last fight was two years ago. He was still in good shape, but his eyes were black and bleary from his drug habit. Since he was a boxer I decided to shape up, like I was going to punch it out with him. He thought he could run all over me. But just when he brought his fists up, I gave him a stinging kick to his kneecap, painful and totally unexpected.

He dropped his hands to his knee, and I gave him a straight jab to the face. He said, "Just hands and first one down loses."

I nodded OK.

Because of his pain he was throwing big punches, telegraphing his intentions. I feinted back, then moved in and hit him in the face. It went on like this for three minutes. He finally got me in the chest, a big punch, and suddenly my body was on fire. But I showed no pain, my adrenaline was flowing, he was starting to slow down and take big breaths. I felt confident I could beat him. I started throwing left-right two punch combinations. I cut him at the top of his left eye. He was still standing. I was also tiring, but he was in much worse shape; his punches getting wider and slower. After another two to the face, he backed away and wanted a breather.

"I need a break and we'll start again in ten minutes."

"No way, you stop now, you lose."

He conceded defeat and the crowd was in shock. I'd beaten the champ. I didn't sleep for the next two days. I thought he would come back and exercise his right to a rematch. He had his excuses in the first encounter, but luckily the fight was enough for him and he wasn't going to threaten me with trouble again. Sergei was amazed and so was the doorman.

Forced Out

I felt more and more alone in Mr. Choong's club. My partner, Robin and Mr. Choong had forgotten their earlier difficulties and were now very chummy. They had regular meetings and lunches together to which I wasn't invited. On the last day of the month, I was asked to a 6 p.m. meeting with Mr. Choong. I was right on time and he was right to the point.

"Joe, I've been offered thirty percent of the turnover by the Chinese boys who say they can run the room and grow the business."

He was getting twenty percent from me currently. The offer of thirty percent from the Chinese sounded genuine. He might want me to match that offer or he could be forcing me out.

"Now I like you and Robin, Joe, but business is business. Because I'm an honest man and you've got a solid reputation. I'm happy to stand by you. If you can match that thirty percent, I'll continue with you and Robin. My partners think that thirty percent is reasonable. So, what do you think, Joe?"

"Well, I've got to be honest as well, Mr. Choong. I think you and your partners are scavengers. Leaches. I came here just four months ago. I had a plan to build a business, and you weren't confident, and you wanted your $10,000 a month, whether or not I made that much. After just three weeks, you wanted twenty percent."

"But you were making…"

"I'm talking now. You're now making five times what you expected to make, and you want to squeeze me for even more?

Well, fuck you! Let's go back to the $10,000 a month." I knew as the words were spitting out of my mouth that my offer was outrageous, but I hated the situation he'd put me in.

He looked at me like I was a simpleton and said, "This is my fucking place, you are nothing here."

"Sure, it's your place, but I'm not giving you and the partners thirty percent. You shouldn't have got twenty. I can go down the road and start back up again." I said, waving my hand in the rough direction of thirty other casinos that could do with my help. Mr. Choong turned his back on me and walked out, red-faced, and breathless.

I found Robin and told him the story. Robin wasn't much help, just saying it was my decision, it was up to me. I called Sergei and told him I needed to see him right away.

Sergei wanted me to swallow my pride and give Mr. Choong what he wanted. "You can't stop now, Joe, everybody wants this place to continue, just give him the thirty percent."

"Even if I do, he's still making less than half of what I'm making."

"Exactly Joe. And only you and I know that. And we'll keep it that way."

I'd already made my mind up not to give in. "I'm not giving him 30 percent."

On the first of the month, I arrived at the club to find twelve security guys there. Mr. Choong was marching me out. "Take your stuff and don't come back. You've got nothing to do with me anymore."

I went to the cabinet, opened it, and said to Robin, "We're finished here. Call the dealers and tell them not to come in today. Take the loan book and the cash float." The loan book was the record of who owed us money. That money was owed to me personally. I'd chase those debts myself once I was settled at a new club and had some power behind me.

I got my personal stuff out of the cabinet and turned around. Robin hadn't moved. It was just me that was being marched. "Joe, I've worked too hard to quit now. I'm staying. I can run the room and Mr. Choong can have the thirty percent."

"Robin, where's your loyalty to me? We can set up another place together, you and I."

He wouldn't look me in the eye. "I'm sorry Joe. Mr. Choong and the partners have asked me to stay."

I was disgusted at this turn of events. Everyone had turned on me. I just walked out.

After a few hours of solitary thinking. I rang Sergei. I had repaid him the $40,000 loan by now, and he'd enjoyed a few weeks of the bonus $1,000 payments on top of that. He wouldn't be getting any more of those. Sergei was furious. "What the fuck were you thinking, Joe? You should have given him the thirty percent; you were still making good money. Now you've got nothing."

"I've got my pride, Sergei, and I've got my honour. And that's everything. I'm not getting pushed around and I'm not getting squeezed by anyone."

"You're not even 21 years old, and you're talking like this. And now you can't pay me either."

"I've already repaid you your money, plus interest, plus several weeks of $1,000 bonus money. Robin's running the whole show now. He didn't want to leave. That's loyalty for you. Loyalty! Nobody gives it to me."

"I'll tell you something, young man. In this life, you only get loyalty when people fear you, or when they need you and they can't do without you. Life's tough. Your partner, Robin, the guy who stayed. He's the smart one. That's the smart play."

I immediately began looking for a new place, somewhere nearby, where I could punish Robin and Mr. Choong for their betrayal. Sergei was by my side and wanted to finance my new venture. He knew I had a talent for this business. He wanted a piece of my action and he wanted to be my advisor.

The Aussie Mob

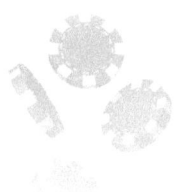

I knew a place run by the old guard, the original Wiseguys of Kings Cross. The head of the group was a famous well-connected gangster who had friends in the police, the judiciary, you name it. If he stayed smart, he was untouchable. My problem was I couldn't deal directly with him. He'd been shot in the eye and was recovering. He was way too busy to meet with a little-known poker operator like myself. So, I had to go through his lieutenants, so to speak. I wasn't on good terms with them however, the underlings knew I could make them money and they knew I could grow their business.

After a few days I was given the green light to start an old club back up, which the Aussie Mob had never done well with before. My offer was five grand per week, they provide the doorman but had no say in any of the other staff. Everything else in the place came under me. They agreed to my terms; not that that meant much in any of my other ventures.

The first week, half of my old costumers came in. That was a good result. My old partner Robin had learned well and was still running a good game for Mr. Choong, so some of the players didn't make the move. The Chinese had teamed up with Mr. Choong and were giving him the thirty percent he was seeking. But my new place was doing well, and the Chinese feared it. On the third night a Chinese player came in, to check out my new place and see who was playing there. He would later pressure my players to stop playing and go back to Mr. Choong's. Anyhow the scout they sent owed me money; $8,000, which had been outstanding for three months. I asked him "Do you have that money you owe me, and why do you keep coming here if you're not playing?" I knew the answer already. I just wanted to see his reaction. He was in no mood to back down.

"Fuck you. I work for Karate Ken, talk to him."

Karate Ken was a feared standover man. He'd been in and out of jail but was back on the streets. He didn't belong to the Chinese mobs, they hired him now and then as muscle on special projects. Nobody was dumb enough to mess with him.

"I didn't give Karate Ken $8,000, I gave it to you." I grabbed him by the neck and escorted him out, telling him in no uncertain terms that if he came in here again, he'd better have my money. If I crossed paths with him on the street, I'd smack him around until I got it.

The next day Karate Ken himself came into the club while I was out. He sat down at a table to wait for me. The doorman phoned me and told me that Karate Ken was looking for me. I promised to be on site within an hour. When I got in, Ken jumped off his chair saying he needed to talk to me. I moved him to the top of the stairs, out of sight of everyone in the main room.

"What's up, Ken?"

"You hit one of my boys yesterday. He told me all about it. He tells me he owes you money."

"Correct so far."

"Well, if you want that money, try getting it out of me!"

"Why? Why would I want to get it off you? I'll get it off him, I already told him that. It's his debt."

"You want to be a tough guy now, Joe, is that it?"

The doorman came upstairs to see what was happening in this escalating situation. Ken and I were facing off, with the doorman right behind me. Suddenly it was on. Ken head-butted me, getting me right in the nose. Blood came spurting out as I immediately tackled him hard against the wall. I was in a good position to hurt him. His Karate skills were useless in a tight close situation. I soon had him pinned to the floor. I had weight advantage and a strength advantage over him. As I crushed him, my own security, my own doorman, grabbed me from behind and pulled me of him. Ken got to his feet and rewarded me with a strong kick to my guts.

The doorman told Ken to leave as the blood continued gushing from my nose. I wanted to follow him outside and finish the business. The doorman stopped me. This wasn't going well. I had no one on my side. The doorman had seen what was going to happen and had intervened when I had Ken pinned.

Half an hour later I went outside to look for Karate Ken. I found him easily enough. He was in one of the Chinese poker rooms, boasting about how he had hit me in the head and kicked me in the guts.

"I'm back, Ken, let's finish this outside."

He said he couldn't. He was out on parole and couldn't risk being arrested on the street and sent back to prison. Instead, he sent three of his boys outside to take me on. They were young boys, 60 to 70 kilos each, five foot eight inches tall. I had a big weight advantage, strength advantage, and probably better fighting skills. I'd had these fights back before in school, three against one. The trick is to take one of them out straight away and then attack a second immediately after. That's how this confrontation played out. I got the first guy right under his chin with my first punch, he wasn't getting up anytime soon. The other two came at me from different sides, trying to blind side me. I attacked the second guy with everything I had, with the third guy getting some punches to the side of my head while I was doing so. I took three hits from him before the second guy was out of action and I could give him proper attention. Karate Ken was watching from above and called the third guy in before he could get what was coming. A big crowd had gathered, luckily none of them policemen. I was a mess; with a broken nose from the headbutt, a black eye, sick to my stomach, but I'd won. My boxing career was now 2-2-0 with two knockouts and a technical knockout against the ex-boxer, but I'd lost my appetite for fist fights. Maybe I could retire undefeated.

    The next day I patched up my wounds and returned to the poker room like nothing had happened. The Aussie Mob knew Ken well. Ken had brought some new Asian gamblers to their casinos, although the guys Ken introduced had run off owing debts, so his gambling contacts weren't that high value after all. This was the same problem I had with Ken's scout who still owed me $8,000.

Chinese Gang Bang

The Chinese had a unique way of getting rid of white guys who didn't have any back up. They got their target outside on the street, then twenty to thirty of them swarmed him like a bunch of killer bees. The attackers were young Chinese in their twenties. Seven or eight of the guys stabbed the victim and hit him with meat cleavers and blunt objects. It was fascinating and sickening at the same time. Most of the time the victim would be dead in a few minutes. By the time the police arrived the victim was comatose in a pool of his own blood. Witnesses would report that he'd been attacked by a team of Chinese. The attackers then went underground; spreading to all parts of Australia, growing moustaches, dyeing their hair, changing their appearances, and staying away for six months.

The police would eventually find and arrest half of the attackers. Witnesses would have trouble identifying who was Hu. When the murder case came to court, years later, the attackers all had reasons for being at the murder. Some were watching, some had thrown punches but never stabbed, a few even said they were trying to stop the attack. If any of the gang had died since the attack, the Chinese would all say that guy had been the murderer who had delivered the fatal blow. The best police were able to do was put a dozen of them in jail for a year on lesser charges like assault and battery. I called it the Chinese Gang Bang, and I'd seen it happen twice before.

By the end of the second week, the Aussie Mob Club was booming, and the Chinese clubs were suffering. I was more than a thorn in their side, they were feeling me like a skewer through their cheek. Their business was down probably by eighty percent.

The gangsters had a good operation going. Plenty of their crew had jobs in the cardroom, and it was all because of what I'd established. But they couldn't leave it alone. Someone came up to me and said that next week they were putting in two blackjack tables. Blackjack was illegal under the skill/chance gambling laws, but twenty-one, where a player acts as bank against the other players, was allowed. Blackjack was the game played, but at the first hint of a raid or an undercover cop, the dealers changed the game to twenty-one. Baccarat is another card gambling game that can be played as a house game or player-as-bank.

I now received a warning. A Chinese friend warned me that the Chinese game runners would try to corner me outside. I was to be the next victim of a Chinese Gang Bang. He suggested I carry a gun, loaded at all times, ready to go. I bought a Colt 45 Chrome, a powerful handgun, sturdy, clean and reliable. I went out to the open country to have a few practice shots with it. It was amazing; scarily accurate. It was a big weapon, easily seen, which sometimes helps. When bad people see you're got a gun, they leave you alone and you don't have to use it. It's less helpful when the police can see you're carrying.

At the end of the fourth week, the Australian Mob put the squeeze on. The asked me to double my payments, to $10,000 a week. What a bunch of fuckers. It was the same old story. The Double Bay Chinese underpaid me and made me train my replacements. The Italian robbed my money from his safe. Mr. Choong went from our agreement of $10,000 a month to twenty percent, then he wanted thirty. As soon as business increases, everyone ups their take. But I couldn't fight the whole Sydney underworld. Sergei and his money could get me up and running time and again, but keeping control of a successful poker room at agreed payment rates were proving impossible.

So, I said to the Aussie Mob, leave it for two weeks at the current rate of $5,000 a week, and then if I continue, I'll make up the shortfall. $10,000 a week in 1986 was a lot of money.

By now I was talking directly with the number one guy of the Sydney underworld. I hadn't met him in person, but we'd spoken on the phone a few times and he was pleased with the casino's success. I sensed he was unhappy about asking me for the extra money so soon after we'd opened; and that his lieutenants had put him up to it.

My Chinese friend came in and gave me a second tip-off. "Joe when you leave here in the morning, they're going to make a move on you. Be prepared. Good luck." I was prepared. I had a big leather jacket with a large inside pocket. The Colt was easy to pull out of this pocket yet couldn't be easily seen from outside. I worked that night as normal. I think the doormen knew something was going on. They acted differently that night, not saying hello or smiling as I came in. A couple of Chinese from the opposition clubs came in that night, not to see how good our business was or who our customers were, but to check that I was there and that I was alone.

It came time to leave the club. It was do or die. I had a plan. I'd stay in areas that were well lit, shoot at least two of the Chinese before they could swarm me, and run into a nightclub 100 meters down the road, holding the rest at bay from the doorway. If I could hold out for ten minutes, the cops could arrive, and I'd throw the gun down and give myself up.

I said goodnight to upstairs security and walked down the stairs to the street door. Our doormen knew I was to be the next Chinese Gang Bang victim. But they didn't know that I knew that too, and that I was carrying a loaded 45 in my jacket. When I got to the bottom, I showed our doormen my gun and cocked it. "I know what's waiting for me out there, and I never asked any of you weak cunts to help me."

Outside the club I took ten steps down the road and saw groups of Chinese at every angle. There was a dozen across the road, ten of them fifty meters behind me and another ten at the bus stop. I was never going to reach the nightclub. My best chance was to shoot two of them and hope they'd disperse. If I waited until they charged, it would be way too late. Even if I managed to shoot a couple, they'd still swarm me.

Just as I aimed at some of the Chinese in front of me, the three doormen ran out of the club, screaming, "Stop! Stop! He's got a gun!" They ran towards me. "Joe, come back upstairs." So, I did. One of the lieutenants had told the head guy in the organisation. The head guy, hearing from the doorman that I was armed, told them to warn the Chinese and get them to call of the attack.

It was acceptable for me to be gang banged. But neither side wanted me to take out a few Chinese along the way, which would bring the law crashing down onto the Cross and cause all the casinos to be shut down again for a long time, maybe forever. There was to be a clean killing or no killing. My actions took the clean killing option away, so there would be no killing tonight.

I was escorted back upstairs and made to wait for the head boss; the untouchable Australian gangster. He had recovered from his shooting. I'd never met him before, though I'd seen him on the TV and seen him from a distance. I had talked to him on the phone a few times. It was now three in the morning. He arrived twenty minutes later.

"Joe. Nice to meet you in person. My name is George."

"I know who you are, Mr. Goodman."

"Please call me George. Now Joe, that was quite a commotion tonight, wasn't it? Why were those Chinese out there trying to kill you?"

Because I'm hurting their business and one of your guys gave the OK for the hit. "George, you know more than me. I hear you're a smart man, you've been around a long time. I'm very good in my business. I'm successful and players like to come to the poker games I run. The Chinese have been making a fortune from the players for many years, and now I come along, and they have no business."

"Yeah, they're hurting, but if they knew that we were behind you, they'd leave you alone and you would be OK."

"Maybe they would leave me alone. But why don't they know you're behind me? Don't you have already? I pay you $5,000 a week. You're running the blackjack tables, and I'm paying you $900 a day for your people on the door. That's what we agreed. That's a business you'd want to safeguard and keep running. If it's not making you enough, just tell me and I'll quit."

"You shouldn't have knocked us back when we asked you for ten thousand last week. Joe, you're making twenty to thirty thousand a week and giving us five. That's a bit greedy, wouldn't you agree?"

"No, I'm giving you twelve grand a week; don't forget the nine hundred dollars a day for your doormen who were quite prepared to watch the Chinese chop me up. I'm not greedy,

George. If I agree to ten thousand a week, next month it'll be fifteen thousand, then twenty thousand, until I'm not making anything myself. Where does it stop?"

"We can do this without you. Everyone can be replaced, Joe. We can run the poker room by ourselves."

"No you can't. You can run the room for two weeks and then your players will leave, and they'll come to my next place. Look at what happened to Mr. Choong's room. If you go it alone, this place will shut down like it was four weeks ago. All of your guys, your boys, people hate them and they're useless."

"You'd better not say that to them."

"I'm saying it to you. Listen, after four weeks, I would have agreed to the ten thousand a week, if I was asked politely and not stood over."

George laughed. Polite negotiations were rare in his world. "I like you Joe, but you've only been around two or three years. My other guys, maybe people hate them, but they would kill for me and take a bullet for me."

"Murder's not my thing, George, in either direction. I'm through with this. Thanks for stopping the carnage outside but this city is too tough for me."

"To be honest with you, Joe, I'm surprised you're still alive. I kept asking my boys ‚who has he got behind him?' and they all said ‚nobody'. I laughed at that, I thought that's impossible. Every week for the last two years people were complaining to me about you. And I kept asking myself how is he still in business? How is he even still alive?"

Wow, people were talking about me to George Goodman, for years… That's quite an achievement. "I think it's time for me to go George, go back to Perth that is. I'm exhausted. I can't do this anymore."

"But if you can meet us at ten thousand a week from the club, we'll have your back. I'm prepared to lock in that rate for a year. No further increases."

"Someone will take me out, sooner or later. Maybe even one of your boys, on the make and ready to move up in the organisation. You'd be sad for a week then you'd move on. I hate to say no, but I'm leaving this business."

"I can't stop you, Joe. But if you quit now, and this place closes down, you will never run anything in Sydney again."

"That's fine by me. I wish I'd met you earlier, George, you're the best of all of them. Thanks for your help tonight. And don't worry, I won't be opening or running any more poker rooms in Sydney."

I shook his hand. He wasn't going to beg me to keep on running the club. But he was sad I was leaving.

THE BOOKIE

My First Million

A few weeks later I was back in Perth. The gambling clubs there were terrible. At one of them the doormen demanded tips from winning players on their way out and slapped them if they refused. Unsurprisingly they lost their players and were soon out of business.

I now had a name, Australia-wide, not as a gangster but as a gaming operator. I also had a lot of money. Underground gambling had just about shut down in Perth, which now had a legal casino.

Many of the old-time gamblers now had nowhere to play. The legal casino, Burswood, was very choosy about who they let in. They didn't want a whiff of scandal or criminal activity inside. I saw an opportunity to start a poker game. There was a lot of confidence in Perth at the time. The stock market was booming, mining was going well, plenty of people had money. Australia had won the America's Cup yacht race for the first time in 1983, and the defence would be in Perth's harbour suburb of Fremantle in 1987. Cashed-up players were looking for somewhere to play, away from the official Government-licensed casino.

So, I started up a game. On the first night ten people showed up. Two of them were extremely bad players. They played against each other for a full fourteen hours. This was tremendous money for the club; we took $15,000 from them. The second night a man from my past turned up; he'd been a schoolmate of mine all those years ago. He'd just been released from jail; he'd done four years for two armed robberies. He asked me for a job in security. I agreed and I paid him more than the other security guys.

The next night, a big local gambler came in and he wanted to play real big.

"How big?" I asked him.

He wanted to play me one-on-one for $25,000.

Dad was in the club that night and told me to play smaller. I stood my ground. I'd played in some big games in Sydney and I felt that I could take on the Perth gambler and win. I accepted the $25,000 challenge. I won and won and won again. After four hours, I was up four buy ins. A full $100,000. Dad told me to quit now. I'd won big money, but it wasn't mine until the game stopped.

I wasn't having that. "There's no way he can beat me, I'll beat him for everything he's got," I told Dad. After two days I was ahead by over half a million dollars, $525,000 to be exact. Dad, who was the same age as the rich gambler I was thrashing, again tried to get me to stop, especially once the stakes changed to a $100,000 match.

I saw this as an opportunity. Very rarely will you be able to win so much from a rich amateur. My opponent owned some mines and mining was booming. We started to play our $100,000 match. Twenty-four hours later the mining boss was $1.1 million behind and too tired to continue. He conceded defeat. He paid me $600,000 in cash and owed me another $500,000. This game was the biggest game ever played in Australia. I was still in my early twenties and was getting a big reputation.

My schoolmate, now in charge of security, saw all the dollars we were making and asked me for a percentage cut. I settled on five percent of each day's takings, roughly $500 per day. My schoolmate was becoming very jealous of the money I was making. He was also envious of other people looking up to me. He started complaining that we should be partners. After all, he said, he was the one keeping all the bad guys out of the club. He was the one standing up to the bad guys who would otherwise overrun the place. It was the same old story I'd seen in Sydney. The success of my club was causing jealousy and greed in others. Hopefully, this club would turn out differently, but I felt the same bad forces building against me. I resolved to keep the club going for as long as I could.

A local gangster, who'd done jail time with my headof security, now arrived on the scene. He thought he was a lot tougher than he really was. Even so, I didn't want to pick a fight with him. From what I could see, he controlled a lot of the local drug trade. The gangster and my schoolmate were very close and suggested a partnership with me that would give them a much bigger share than they deserved. They really had no idea about gambling. We were all the same age, in our early twenties, and we had a priceless opportunity to make a few million dollars a year. without competition, as the only alternative to Burswood.

After two months their jealousy boiled over. I'd offered them very good terms to help run the operation as a partnership, but they refused and were secretly planning to open a gambling room themselves. Rumours were that I would be bashed and forced to close down. My schoolmate had changed his allegiance without telling me. They planned to let in some criminals and trash the club. My partners would then start a new venue down the road and become the new game in town. It was so petty. Instead of taking a good share of a thriving business, my schoolmate had to stick the knife in. He was jealous of the money I was making, even though he could make great money himself, just by staying part of my business. He really had it in his mind that he deserved an equal share.

My schoolmate made sure he was nowhere to be found on the night of the attack. Some obvious undesirables were let in. Criminals came in two by two, as though my club was a Noah's Ark for lowlife. I went downstairs to see what the story was on the door. There was only one doorman tonight, the other was running late and I was told my schoolmate wasn't corning in. There was nothing for me to do but prepare for the coming storm. Dad was playing in the club that night and I knew that if he saw me attacked, he'd join in no matter how many people were against me.

Ten minutes later a gangster and two guys asked for a conversation. I was told to shut down immediately. "Close this fucking place up," I was told.

"That's not going to happen," I replied. I then made the mistake of letting down my guard, just for a second. As I turned my back, the gangster, a local legend in the boxing world, hit me from behind, stunning me. The noise attracted Dad's attention.

"What's going on Joe?"

"Nothing Dad, no big deal. It's under control. I'll be with you in a minute."

"Someone king-hit Joe", Dad was told.

"Everything's all right, Dad. It's just business. See you soon."

Once we stopped the game, the players were allowed to leave unharmed and Dad and I left with no further injuries. They didn't damage the building or the equipment but I was told not to try re-open the club.

My security schoolmate turned up twenty minutes later. "What's going on, what happened?" he asked me.

"You know exactly what happened, good luck trying to run your own club. I'm through with this."

My schoolmate had washed his hands of the attack, but I knew I'd been betrayed and that he'd sold me out. It was all over for me. These guys had brains the size of peas. Nobody came to their poker club. Everyone in Australia seemed to think that running a poker club was easy and they could do it themselves. They failed time and time again.

The end of my Perth poker club wasn't that big a deal to me financially; but it was just so disappointing, such a shame. It had only lasted two months and should have run for at least two years. I kept coming up against jealousy and envy in the underworld. It was a jungle, with no rules and no honour. There was jealousy, envy, egos, gossip, and backstabbing. Actually, making money and sharing profits fairly was a long way down on the list, if it was there at all.

On the plus side, I was now a millionaire. The mining boss paid off his final $600,000 by giving me a block of apartments. I'd made more as a poker player than a poker operator, and as a player the hassles were much less. As an operator I had no friends, and anyone could take me out at any time. I was pretty lucky to still be alive. I didn't have any friends I could trust in this business, apart from Sergei who had financed two of my Sydney casinos. Sergei had given me self-belief, that I could make it in this world, at a crucial time of my life.

So now I was simply a player, and the best action was in Sydney. I went back there, simply to play, chill out and have a good time, not to run any more rooms. I didn't want permission from George Goodman to open a venue again, I just wanted to play big poker.

The Player

I'd tried my luck as a player years earlier; between my time as a Double Bay dealer and the Italian room. I was a consistent winner, though I'd never had enough money to play regularly in the biggest games. Now I had that money. I went to some of the top end of town games. You needed $10,000 to sit down at those games. I was now comfortable at these limits. Goodman's gangsters noticed me pretty quickly. They still disliked me, but I was paying their rake along with the rest of the big players. At just twenty-three years of age, I was playing in the biggest games and making much more money than the jealous gangster lowlifes. Goodman himself came into one of the poker clubs, shook my hand, and we had a private chat for fifteen minutes.

"Welcome back to Sydney, Joe. How was your time in Perth?"

"I tried running a room, but my partners screwed me over. Even my mates in Perth don't want me running clubs."

"That's what I heard. I hope you won't be starting anything up around here either. Remember what I told you last time."

"There's no chance of that, George. I'm not going back to that life. I've got some money of my own now. I can play in the big games and make it just as a player. I'll be able to walk around Kings Cross without people trying to take me out. I won't get harassed for bigger and bigger shares of my profits. It's just me now and I report to no-one. "

Goodman understood. We shook hands and he repeated his warning for me not to get involved with running casinos anymore, after I'd walked out on our partnership last year.

Word got around that Goodman had talked to me one-on-one and respected me. It also became known that I had money. Sergei found out that I was back in Sydney and sought me out. When we met, he was full of praise for me. He'd told everyone in the underworld that I'd make it and he felt so proud of me and his part in my success. He offered to be my driver and hang out with me for a few months. He found me a great room in a five-star hotel. It should've cost $300 a night but I got it for $130. I loved it. It was a great place to bring women back. They were always impressed.

Party Time

One day Sergei took me out to breakfast. Dressed to the nines, he picked me up at 8 a.m. Expecting a bacon and eggs breakfast, I was dressed in jeans, a denim shirt and sneakers. We were joined by two Russian girls. The girls wore diamonds, evening gowns and high heels. They were beautiful girls, about five years older than me. Sergei told the girls the story of our time together; the bench in Kings Cross, his $40,000 investment and how I was able to quickly repay it at $4,000 a week. We went to a classy Chinese restaurant. We ate lobster fresh from the fish tank with black bean and chili, along with abalone and prawns. For drinks, we had two bottles of vodka and some orange juice and ice on the side. There are worse ways to have breakfast.

We'd been eating and talking for an hour when I needed a bathroom break. Sergei followed me and pushed something into my pocket.

"What's that, Sergei?" Sergei rolled his eyes.

"Ummm it's cocaine, Joe. The good stuff. Colombian and un-cut."

I'd had cocaine a few times before, but it had never done that much for me. It kept me awake which was sometimes helpful in long poker games, but it also affected my judgment which is the last thing you need at high stakes. Today was a party day though. Sergei got his own coke out and he and I snorted it in the toilets and returned to the Russian girls ready for further action. Sergei's coke was the best I'd ever had. My whole mouth went numb and my front teeth were tingling. I felt fresh, five years younger, and ready for anything. The coke in my pockets would be good for later.

Sergei chatted in Russian to the girls, who were starting to make eyes at me. They looked like cute puppy dogs. The one I fancied, slightly taller than her friend, pushed herself onto me and started rubbing my inner thigh up and down. If the Chinese restaurant guys noticed any of this, they discreetly saw nothing. It was feeling nicer and nicer.

"What's going on?" I asked her. She just smiled and then suddenly my whole cock was in her hand. In poker terms, she had the nuts. Her friend leaned over the table, giving me a fine view of her fantastic breasts. They were huge, firm, and all natural. Decent action in what I thought was a conservative Chinese restaurant. I was teased by the girls for another five minutes and then it was their turn for a bathroom break.

"Wow, Sergei, those girls were all over me. Guess what the tall lady had in her hand?"

"She had your cock in her hand, Joe. But what did she have in her other hand?"

"Her other hand? What do you mean?"

"Check your pockets, Joe".

I checked them. The coke Sergei had given me was gone. The Russian girls had got what they were after. "Fuck, I thought those girls really liked me."

"They do Joe, relax. At the moment you're the third most important thing in their life. The most important is the coke. Next most important is each other; they're lesbians and in love with each other. But don't worry, they like to party."

I told him I liked the taller girl, who had grabbed my cock. Sergei said I was in with a real chance there.

The girls returned five minutes later and were buzzing.

"So how was it girls?" I asked them as they giggled.

"Yeah it was real good," they told me.

"So what do you girls do when you're not having fun?"

"We came to Australia as students two years ago," my favourite said. "We really need to get married soon; because we want to stay in this country and get married. Oh, are you married?"

"No, I'm too young for that. But both of you are so nice and I've had such a great time all day. It's midday now and I'd like to show you my hotel room, Lina."

I thought the girls deserved some compensation for their time and I gave the other girl, Oksana, ten hundred dollar bills. She didn't like the transaction.

"What do you think we are? Prostitutes?"

"No, no, you're students, right?"

In a low voice Lina murmured to Oksana to please take my money. Oksana was her senior partner. Oksana pulled an offended face, as though she was lowering her standards in taking my dirty cash, but the money was in her purse soon enough.

Lina now grabbed my arm, and we were ready to rock and roll. I left $900 on the table for the meal, the drinks and a sizeable tip for the discreet Chinese.

Lina and I were soon back in my hotel room. It was only a five-minute walk from the restaurant. She was impressed with my luxury standard of living and asked me how long I'd be around for.

"A few more months" I told her.

She rolled out another line of cocaine and began cutting up the dust so she could sniff it. She then went into the bathroom and undressed, not troubling herself to close the door behind her. It's remarkable how sexy it is just to watch a woman undress naturally. Lina was tall with a perfect physique topped off by great breasts; larger than average and totally real. If you think of Maria Sharapova with even better tits, you'd be on the money. I undressed too and joined her in the shower; which was a huge shower that could fit four people easily. I soaped up her body in the shower and was too worked up to wait for towelling off afterwards.

We made love in the shower. As I entered from behind, I could see her face in the mirror and she was very happy with this turn of events. Afterwards we washed and dried ourselves. I needed to sleep, I was booked for a big private poker game at 10:30 tonight and needed my rest. She kissed me and held me as I drifted off to sleep.

I woke up hours later, refreshed, and told Lina to stay in the room, watch a movie and order anything she liked from room service. I'd be away for the night, but I'd be back before sunrise.

The High Life

Now it was time to win some money at the poker game. When I arrived, I knew everyone and they all knew and respected me, young as I was. I was being treated so well. I was known to be wealthy and a close friend of George Goodman. The poker that night was easy money, after six hours I was winning $8,000 and another player was ahead $20,000. One player was down $40,000. The rest of the money was with the staff and the game-runners. I noticed a hot waitress, who I'd seen before and quite fancied. She used to date one of the mob's lieutenants and never gave me a smile. But tonight, she actually placed her hand on my left shoulder, accidentally pressing her breasts onto my back, and asked me if I'd like something to drink, with a husky whisper in my ear.

"Yeah, I'll have a coffee with milk on the side" I told her. I watched her leave to prepare the coffee; admiring her tight dress, showing off a great arse, and her high heels. She looked back to ask if I wanted sugar, winking at me that she knew I was ogling her fabulous body.

The game finished soon afterwards. The host thanked me for keeping my appointment because if I hadn't come tonight the game wouldn't have gone ahead.

"No problem at all, anytime you need a player you can call me." If the game stayed this good, I'd ploy in it whenever I could.

My waitress came back with the coffee, placing it on a small side table behind the poker table, and again pressed her breasts onto me. This time there was no doubt that the contact was intentional. I pulled out a $100 bill and tipped her. Drinks were provided free at the games, many players tipped $5 or $20, but $100 was unheard of. "Thank you so much for your work tonight," I told her, acknowledging her special efforts.

I called Sergei and asked him to meet me at a nearby 24-hour café in an hour. He was there bang on time, shaved, in a new suit and well-polished shoes. I was impressed by his presentation at 5 a.m.

"Well Joe, what's up?" It was rare for me to call on him at this hour.

"Sergei, I'm flying right now, people are looking at me differently now that I've got money. And that Russian girl, Lina, is absolutely fantastic. Tonight I won $8,000. People were lining up to shake my hand and congratulate me, and the waitress was winking at me and pressed her body against me a few times. Life is good!"

"Well, that's how it is, Joe, when you've got a name and you've got the money to back it up. People heard what you did in Perth, beating that guy one-on-one for over a million dollars. You need to keep your head screwed-on straight though. You're a target now."

This is what I needed to hear from Sergei and why I'd got him out of bed for an overnight coffee. I needed someone to tell me to stay well grounded. I knew that I couldn't spend my whole life spending big on partying and playing around like this. As fast as my life was running right now, I needed someone to remind me that it needed to slow down.

"Proceed with caution, Joe. The money you're winning is coming from the losers. If you get too big, and it costs others too much, those guys can destroy you. As for women, well that's easy. Don't get yourself attached at your young age. I suggest you travel the world for a few years. You'll see a lot and you'll learn a lot. You'll have all kinds of women. And I guarantee you, you'll finish with a Russian woman."

"I hope so. Someone like Lina would be ideal. She was fantastic, the best I've ever had."

"Forget Lina. She's OK, but I'd only score her an eight out of ten."

"Eight? Your standards are high, Sergei."

"Come to Moscow one day, Joe, then you'll meet the nines and the tens."

As he drove me back to the hotel, I saw a giant calculator in the console of Sergei's car, connected with a wire to the cigarette lighter plug of the car. I had to know what it was.

"This is a mobile phone Joe, the first one in all of Australia. You can make calls from anywhere with this, and people can call you as well. The police can't tap the calls and they won't know where you are."

"You mean I can make calls on this?" My mind was abuzz with the possibilities and the potential. "This is great, this is the future. Lots and lots of people are going to need one of these."

"Everyone will need one in a few years. I can get ten of these into the country, and rent each one out at $200 a day."

Mobile plans are cheaper nowadays, but at least Sergei's plan was simple and uncomplicated.

"I've got a great idea for these."

"What's your great idea. Joe?"

"I can't tell you, Sergei."

We laughed. He'd needed my business plan all those years ago, on the park bench, when he'd loaned me the $40,000 for my poker room. I didn't need his money now, and I could afford to keep my ideas to myself.

Sergei dropped me off at the hotel, giving the a slip of paper with his mobile number written on it. "Put it in your shirt pocket. Joe." As I did that, it bumped into the cocaine that Sergei had snuck in there during the drive. The man was a magician.

Lina hadn't been shy in taking advantage of room service while I was out winning at poker. There were empty plates of food everywhere. She was eating pancakes and black caviar when I entered. She suggested I have some too, so I ordered some from room service, which they told me would be delivered in twenty five minutes. There was time to do another line of coke.

Lina was pleased with this and came over to indulge. She was wearing just the hotel bathrobe and as she was sniffing the coke, the bathrobe opened pleasingly.

The caviar and pancakes arrived at a noticeable cost of $265 plus tax making it close to $290. I put three $100 notes on the folder, though the hotel staff was upset she was only getting a $10 tip. Well, that's life in that business, you're only as good as your last tip.

The caviar didn't really do it for me, the cocaine had killed my appetite. There were only three mouthfuls of caviar, $100 a swallow pretty much. There was cream, onions, and a hard-boiled egg on the side which I left untouched.

Sergei had told me that the other Russian girl, Oksana, was jealous and worried about Lina, and that we had to call her and give her an update.

"Joe, is Lina OK?"

"Of course she is Oksana. We're living it up here."

"Joe, you didn't introduce her to any other women did you?"

I had so much easy cash that I could have afforded to pay another girl to have a threesome with Lina and me. Oksana wanted to be the only woman in that triangle.

"No no, just me. She's been with me all day."

"I want to come and check she's OK."

Lina was listening in to the conversation and didn't like this idea but we had to go through with it.

"Sure, come and join us. Hilton City Hotel, Room 1415"

"I'll be there in forty-five minutes."

Lina was upset and said Oksana was domineering and would spoil our fun. Oksana arrived soon enough, fresh as a daisy, dressed in a track suit as though she was on her way to the gym. She and Lina embraced, they were genuinely in love, though as Lina had said Oksana was controlling. Oksana was dazzled by the hotel room, the harbour views, and the new line of coke I offered her.

We were on the bed soon enough, Oksana and I on the sides, Lina in the middle. Oksana was running the show and was ordering Lina around in Russian. Lina was obeying, a passive pussy cat. The hotel TV had Kim Basinger stripping, in *Nine and a Half Weeks*, as Joe Cocker sang *You Can Leave Your Hat On*. Oksana was watching closely, then suddenly yelled out "Suka" - the Russian word for "Bitch." She grabbed Lina's head, forcing her down on her pussy. I stopped watching the film and instead saw Lina's head bobbing up and down under the blankets. Oksana had a mean look on her face, biting her lip as Lina pleasured her. She saw I was watching the action, even though I tried not to make it too obvious. She pulled some of the blanket away, so I could see Lina's face and tongue working on Oksana's pussy. This live show was better than any movie I'd ever seen, and I'd be joining in at the right time. Oksana could see my erection and was just reaching her climax herself, from Lina's wonderful tongue. After a powerful shudder, Oksana relaxed and Lina caught her breath, too scared to say a word.

Again, Oksana yelled "Suka" and directed her slave Lina to help me out with my issue, to make me comfortable. Lina had removed all of Oksana's clothes under the blanket and now used her stripping talents on me. I laid down on the bed and Lina's mouth was soon over my cock. Oksana was watching Lina go to work on me, enjoying it almost as much as I was. As Lina kept the sucking up, Oksana took off her t-shirt, her last remaining clothes, and started rubbing her firm tits in my face. She had fantastic tits, her hours in the gym had kept her firm and made her powerful. She thanked me for keeping an eye on Lina, quite sarcastically, to show me she was in control of the younger Russian, not me. After a few more minutes I came right into Lina's sucking mouth. She kept at it for another minute, making sure she had all my cum in her mouth, not spilling a drop of it on the sheets. I was amazed.

Oksana yelled to her to get a shower ready; Lina jumped off the bed and without trying to spit any sperm out, turned on the shower and fiddled with the temperature of the water for a while.

"This is how we do it in Russia, Joe," Oksana told me. "But just this one time for you. I'm sure you enjoyed it."

The ladies left soon after with a generous parting gift from me. Adding yesterday's breakfast, the payments to Oksana, and Lina's caviar room-service habit, together I realised I'd spent

$3,500 in the last 24 hours. Was it worth it? Yes! Oh yes, it was! Don't do it every day of your life, but a day like this one was absolutely worth it.

Appearance is Everything

The next day I met Sergei for lunch. Fabulously dressed as always, he wasn't happy with my clothes. He said my jeans and denim shirt made me look like a Westie; an unsophisticated native of Sydney's western suburbs like Blacktown and Penrith. Well, I was born in Perth. You can't get further west than that.

"Joe, you're a millionaire now, it's time you started looking decent. It'll help you at the poker tables too, I just know it."

He took me to a famous Italian menswear shop, De Ferrari Moda (Italian for "The Ferrari of Fashion"). There were no 70% off sales or discounts here, everything was the best of the best and priced accordingly. Sergei asked the tailor to pull out three suits. I was measured up, and it's nicer when a tailor does it and not a gangster; a tough guy sizes you up in a different way. I tried on the suits. They were fantastic and so comfortable. The shirts were even better. Everything was made from natural fabrics, cotton, and wool. No plastic, polyester or nylon here. In the dressing room I checked the price tag: $1,150. This was crazy. The next suit I tried was $1,450, and it was even better. I'll take that one, I said.

"He'll take all three," Sergei said with authority. "Also, the three ties, five pairs of socks and the five Armani shirts."

I tried to protest but Sergei talked me into it and soon I was in for two pairs of Italian leather shoes as well. My old dressing habits were still with me though. I got a looser pair of shoes than Sergei liked, simply because they wore better with my jeans.

The final purchase was an overcoat; not something I'd worn before but once I tried it on, it looked fantastic. Sydney isn't that cold, even in winter, but this overcoat looked so good that I was getting it. The tailor took all our purchases into the back room and came back with pen and paper and a long list of figures which tallied up to no less than $10,750. I was shocked; this was the price of a new Holden. I could buy a new car or some very classy clothes. Sergei negotiated a discount to $10,000 if we paid in cash. We had the cash.

Sergei told me outside that while this was a lot of money to spend on clothes, I was my own boss now and I had to look the part. He didn't want me looking like the other guys on the scene who wore the same suit and shoes for ten years.

The Sauna

"I've got a treat for you today, Joe," Sergei told me one Monday. "There's some people for you to meet and an old friend of yours. We're going to a sauna."

The sauna was on the 20th floor of a new hotel. There were four jacuzzies, and a wet and dry sauna - it was well kitted out. It was a favourite meeting place for the Aussie Mob. Sergei told me not to talk to anyone. He and I would sit together. If people wanted us, they'd approach us. They used eucalyptus scents in the sauna which cleared my sinuses. We put on robes and shorts and went to the lounge to await our massages. Sergei ordered fresh juice and Chinese tea. I was totally relaxed and sleepy even though it was just after midday. Twenty minutes later George Goodman himself came in, with a party of eight associates. I knew most of them already. They were his generals and underlings, many of whom I'd had run-ins with in the old days.

They sat ten metres away. As Sergei had told me, I waited for them to approach me. I didn't wait long. George called me over and introduced me to the generals: Bruce, Lenny and Charlie. I knew their names of course, but it was different once George introduced me. George presented me as a smart young man, a good earner, and now a rich man. George's crew had just come from lunch, a retirement lunch for old Bert. Bert had finally had enough, at age 80, and was gracefully leaving the organisation; not an easy thing to do in the underworld. Bert was selling out of his gambling interests and there was an opportunity for someone to take over his share of a gambling club.

"This is a young man's game," George said. "I wish I was only 23 years old, like Joe here." George was only 51 years old, but looked older; he'd seen and done a lot in his life. George's party of generals and yes-men agreed with him. The only young people anywhere nearby were the guards fifty metres away; they were new guys on the scene. They were Lebanese or Syrian, certainly Arabic, and they were starting to make waves in the underworld. They didn't look happy that someone of my young age was already friendly and closely connected with George.

"So, you know Joe, we meet here every Monday. At 1.30 p.m., after our golf game. Do you play golf, Joe?"

"No, George, never took it up."

"No problem. Anyway, we're here every week. Come in sometimes and have a chat. You know where to find us."

The generals didn't like this invitation being extended to me but could do nothing about it. I turned to Bert and congratulated him on his retirement. I wondered how he'd stay happy without all the action in his life. Guys in this world didn't become gardeners and take up lawn bowls.

"Well Joe, I'm eighty years old now," Bert told me. "I've done this for sixty years and like George said, it's a young man's game. I lost a lot of money lately and I'd like to enjoy what's left of it, in the time I have remaining on this earth. I'd like to spend some time with my grandchildren and leave them a little something as well."

"You know Joe, Bert's selling his share of the club and the bookmaking business that goes with it," George added. "There's a bit of blackjack and poker, you can play in the poker game if you like but you don't have to. The main focus of the club is SP bookmaking."

Taking bets on horseraces, trotting, and greyhounds was illegal outside of the racetracks and the TAB stores. There were hundreds of secret betting rooms where SP bookmakers took illegal bets. For many Australians betting on the Saturday afternoon races with an SP bookie was their single weekly criminal activity.

I was interested. "How much would you want for your share of the club, Bert?"

"I'd need eighty thousand," he told me.

"Sounds like a good deal, Bert. Let me think about it and get back to you."

"You'll be looked after by our boys Joe," George assured me. I'd have the backing of his mob and the club wouldn't be burnt down or overcharged for protection.

"I'm very interested, but bookmaking is a tricky business. I'll call you tomorrow."

It was time for Sergei and I to have our massage, which gave us some private time together. Sergei warned me that this could be a trap. George could be setting me up. Goodman was one of Australia's biggest horserace gamblers. He'd been warned off racetracks Australia-wide. He'd been photographed in the member's area of Randwick racecourse a few years earlier as the guest of NSW's Chief Magistrate, which caused great embarrassment to the judge as it showed just how well George was connected and how deeply the tentacles of his influence spread.

Once you're warned off racetracks, you can't place legal bets anymore. George wanted to bet and wanted to bet big. Sergei warned me that George could be helping me on my way up, or he might be setting me up for a big fall.

SP Bookmaker

I told George I'd meet him and Bert at the betting shop on Thursday. On the Wednesday, I got ready for my visit. I put on one of my new suits. It wore just as well as it had in the shop. It made me look totally different: serious, businesslike, and older. I went to an electronics shop and bought a miniature tape recorder. It was the size of a paperback book but heavier. I had a plan to see what George's intentions really were in letting me into Bert's bookmaking business. I also went to a carpentry shop and got some adhesive pads. I rigged up the pads on the back of the tape recorder, so that I could stick the tape recorder onto the underside of a table.

I then went to Bert's club, a day earlier than our arranged Thursday meeting. The club was small and quiet. I found a small square table at the corner of the club, ideal for my plan. My plan was to meet George and Bert on the Thursday and bring them to that table, away from the customers and a natural place to have a private chat about me buying Bert's share. I'd then get Sergei to call me on my mobile phone, giving me an excuse to go outside and return 20 minutes later. While I was gone, George and Bert would stay at that table and keep talking about the plan,

and I'd get their true feelings on what they had in mind for me. I'd return to the club from my "urgent business" with Sergei, retrieve the tape recorder, and listen to it later to see what was really in their minds.

The plan worked perfectly. I showed off the mobile phone to George and Bert, explaining how I could use it to take bets even if I wasn't in the club. Sergei called me bang on time, and I left the club for a while as George and Bert stayed at the table, not knowing my tape recorder was under the table saving their private conversation. We spoke a bit longer after I returned, and I asked to stick around to see what business was like that day.

I needed a pretext for retrieving the tape recorder. I asked to recharge my mobile phone; which needed me to hook up a cable to a power point. I plugged the phone charger in close to the table, and managed to safely retrieve my tape recorder.

Back at the hotel, I listened to the recording. As I suspected, they were setting me up. Goodman would place big bets with me. He had fixed horseraces before and still had the talent. Within two months, they estimated, they would win my whole fortune of two million dollars. They'd give me confidence that I was in their gang, that I was one of the group, but then they'd destroy me.

I was disappointed but I'd known others had fallen into this trap before. Many other bookmakers had lost big to George in the past; and they were older, experienced bookmakers. Bert himself had taken some of George's big bets in the last year and had paid a heavy price.

So, I had to come up with a plan. If I simply took George's bets, I risked going broke. I came up with a better way. Something that had never been done before. It was simple. Two mobile phones. One for me and one for my runner. I would take George's bets, and the second after the phone call ended, I'd call my runner and get him to place exactly the same bet with the bookmakers in the betting ring at the racecourse. You get better odds in the betting ring, fixed odds at the time of your bet. The starting price, which I would have to pay George at if his bet won, was normally a bit lower.

When George's bet won, I won too, pocketing the difference between the betting ring price and the starting price. If George's bet lost, he would repay me the amount of the bet at our settlement on Monday. This plan wasn't even illegal. It didn't even seem unethical. I did some research on betting laws. So long as none of the mobile phones were on a racecourse when I made the call or my man received the call, this was all legal.

I needed a runner; quite literally a runner; someone who could get from the street to the betting ring in under a minute. I had just the guy in mind.

Bookie's Runner

I called an Italian friend, Roger, who had worked with me before as my fitness coach. Roger loved gambling and boy, could he run. Some years earlier he'd won Australia's famous professional sprint race, the Stawell Gift. I was in need of his gambling and sprinting talents.

The Stawell Gift is like a horserace run by humans. Once a year, the best sprint runners in Australia meet in the Victorian country town of Stawell. They race to be first across the line, but they don't all run the same distance. The best runners run the full 120 metres. Runners considered less of a chance, start closer to the line and have a shorter distance to race. Racehorses are handicapped by the weight they have to carry. Stawell Gift humans are handicapped by their starting position. The race has a colourful history and over the years there have been betting plunges and good sprinters running slowly in lead-up events to get a better handicap and have a better chance of winning.

With Roger signed on, I rang George to accept his offer of Bert's share in the SP bookies club. George was happy and innocently asked if it was OK if he could bet with me too? I told him yes but limited his bets to $20,000 a race. I didn't want to go broke and neither did I want to win too much of his money. He'd have to bet with me directly, ringing through his bets to my mobile phone.

"Twenty grand a race is fine for now, Joe", George said leaving open the possibility of even bigger bets in future if he could talk me into it. "We settle each Monday at the sauna at

1.30 p.m. My money will always be there. Make sure your money is there if I win."

"No problem, George. Good luck this Saturday and I'll see you on Monday."

So, on Saturday I left a guy at the club to manage the small customer bets. The punters at the club bet with cash and not on credit. There was no chance that the club would be broken by a winning $10,000 bet.

I drove around in a car with my mobile phone, keeping an eye out for police. If I'd taken George's calls in the club, there was a chance of falling victim to a raid or of my scheme being sussed out by someone in the club. George placed his first bet with me, $5,000 on number 3 to win in Race 1. I rang that bet through to Roger, he placed $5,000 on number 3 in the Randwick betting ring. He got fixed odds of 4 to 1 ($5.00). Number 3 won by two lengths. The starting price, the price I had to pay George at, was 7 to 2 ($4.50). Roger collected $20,000 in winnings on this race. George's winnings on this race was $17,500. The $2,500 difference was mine to keep, Typically the best ring price was fifty cents to a dollar more than the starting price. For hot favourites, the best ring price was sometimes just ten cents better or the same as the starting price.

George rang again to make sure I'd pay out on his bet. "Of course, George, you're a valued customer."

"I hope you're not angry, Joe. Don't worry, not all of my bets win."

"No problem George, good luck for the rest of the day. You're up $17,500 so far."

George's horses often shortened in price right before the race. Word on the street was that he fixed some races and gave out "sure-thing" tips to cops, judges, businessmen and friends; making everyone happy and extending his network of influence. The pile of money from everyone in the know following George's tips made the starting price a lot shorter than what Roger got in the ring.

George had a great day that Saturday, placing seven bets for a win of $65,000. Roger was up $77,500 so my profit before expenses was $12,500. I was making over 20% just on the difference between the fixed price and the starting price. In George's eyes, he was sending me broke.

Back at the club, the small-time live punters had suffered a loss, the profit from them was $3,000. I gave the minder $200 wages, and he was happy too.

Monday at the sauna. I came with George's $65,000 and did my best to look hard done by. The yes-men were laughing, and George had a big smile on his face. George thanked me for taking him on and I thanked him for being a good customer and said I'd see him next week.

The second Saturday was outstanding for George. He won $110,000. The starting prices weren't much less that day. I won $15,000 on the difference; still over 10 percent of the winnings. This was proving to be a lot of fun. I had loads of money in the bank in case something happened to Roger and he couldn't on-place George's bets on track for me, but he hadn't let me down on a single bet so far. Roger rang me after each race, he was the best runner I could ask for.

The third week George's horses came in at big odds, he was flying and I made an enormous $90,000 on the difference. I pretended that my bookmaking losses to him were inconsequential, since I was scoring so big in property and on the share market. He had the happy feeling that I could keep taking his bets for a long time. I sensed he didn't want to break me (but would if he had to) and he believed me when I said I was making enough money from other sources. After I handed over his fourth week's winnings, George had a new proposal. I could invest in three young thoroughbreds, yearlings, and George's trainer would manage them. Before long I'd have a good share in three racehorses. George had the know-how and the connections to get the right horses. I agreed; my share cost $80,000 and the others in the scheme were George himself and a hotel owner. This was a good partnership for me; it became known in the underworld that I was a racehorse partner of George's and nobody would mess with me on that basis alone. George was bold enough to go to the yearling sales; he'd been warned off racetracks Australia-wide and probably shouldn't have been so openly involved with the racing industry, but nobody asked him to leave.

The top horses at this auction were being sold for three hundred to four hundred thousand dollars; however when George bid $100,000 for a horse that he wanted there were no other bidders. Either George was buying an unfancied horse, or his influence extended to other buyers; who wouldn't cross him by bidding up the price of the horse he wanted. George got two other horses even cheaper at $40,000 and $50,000. George's horse-trainer, a grizzled old veteran of the game, recommended these horses to hire. We were pleased with our purchases and expected the horses to be racing in 18 months' time.

Saturday at the track. George was winning, I was winning, and even the club was doing well; I had a few small-time customers who were regular losers whose bets I could easily handle myself. Much as I wanted it to, this arrangement couldn't carry on forever. You don't keep putting on big winning bets in the Sydney racetrack betting rings without attracting attention. My runner, Roger, was becoming notorious. Over half of his bets were winning, and the bookies feared him. They called him "The Breeze" - he'd fly in from nowhere and put on huge bets; many of them winners. But he felt he was being watched. He knew that some heavy characters were starting to ask questions about him, and it wouldn't be long before their interest became still more personal and intense.

I doubled Roger's fee to $1,000 a meeting and reminded him that his job was to hit and run; not to stay around the racetrack socialising with other gamblers and draw attention to himself. Roger told me people were asking who he was putting the bets on for, where he got his tips from, and who was behind all of this. I told him to keep his mouth shut, put the bets on and keep to himself.

The Breeze managed to put my bets on for two more weeks. George was now up over one million dollars in the two months I'd been taking his bets. He kept checking with me that the arrangement was OK and that I still had enough money to settle with him each Monday.

I was clearing nearly half as much as George, $450,000, without really risking a dollar of my own money. I was living like a king; staying at my luxury hotel room, eating at the best restaurants, and women were never far away. I had to be focused and on the ball every Saturday for the races, and there were still some poker games to take seriously, but the rest of my week was party time.

It didn't last. Thugs at the racetrack collared Roger, roughed him up, stood over him and asked him some questions. He told them everything. George called me Sunday night to confirm my attendance at Monday's sauna settlement session. "Of course I'll be there, George, I've got your winnings from the weekend," I told him.

I had some time to think about tomorrow's meeting, where I expected I'd be confronted by George about my use of Roger. Sure enough, when I got to the sauna on Monday, a large group of George's gang was with him. I was outnumbered. They were trying to intimidate me and catch me lying. Looking much more confident than I felt, I walked up to them with my bag full of money and a big smile.

"So Joe, let's get straight to the point," George began. "This man Roger, the Breeze, has been making lots of bets at Randwick and Rosehill on Saturdays. Is he working for you?"

"George, it's like this. You bet with me. You win, you get paid, Now this man Roger. Sure, he works for me. So what? What I do is my business, as long as you get paid." This sounded good as I was saying it, so I pushed on. "And I'm not happy with your goons grabbing him and threatening him."

The situation was tense. The mob supporting George were ready to pounce on me if George wanted them to. I was sweating, and not just because this standoff was taking place in a sauna. George thought about what I'd said for two minutes. "All good, Joe. You're a smart boy." Some of the goons were disappointed the situation had eased, but for now George was favourable towards me.

So everyone was happy for now. The club was doing well, and the bookmaking was doing well. I didn't need Roger to on-sell the small cash bets at the club, I could handle that action myself.

Toss the Coins

George then suggested I restart two-up. Two-up was a gold mine for the casinos but hadn't been seen since the skill-game/chance-game changes. I don't know if the game structure had anything to do with it, but two-up players were almost always ex-criminals; volatile and impossible to control. Every now and then, a player would come at the staff with a knife or a gun; it was serious stuff. Still, George had suggested it and I'd proved up to all of his challenges so far. I'd survived the Chinese gang bang, and I'd survived his huge winning racing bets. Handling an unruly two-up game should be well within my capabilities. The gangsters smiled at my boldness in agreeing to run two-up. They all knew the difficulties involved and the trouble that had happened in the past with the game.

So I now had a lot to manage at the club; two-up, poker, and the SP bookmaking. I was now the main gambling operator for George Goodman. He had other mob interests, but for gambling I was his man. The three horses we had a share in were developing well and would be racing in just a few months.

Jealous gamblers and other operators were continually complaining about me to George, behind my back. Some of the stuff they said about me was ridiculous. Once I went to another casino, to pay some money I owed to the owner. I noticed some other customers in this club, who owed my club money, but because of the rule not to chase debts in other clubs, I left them alone. The only thing I did was pay the money that I owed.

Word got around that I'd been at the other club to chase debts. George called and asked if I owed anybody money. I told him no. I'd discharged my debt to the other casino and paid the owner's son the money I owed his dad. This was quickly confirmed.

Lots of people were in George's ear, and none of them wanted to say good things about me. This went on for a whole year. It was all bullshit; nothing was ever proven. Things gradually improved. I finally felt that I belonged in this environment. I no longer felt too young or out of my depth. I had a full understanding of Sydney's underground gaming scene and with George's backing and my own money, I felt that anything was possible.

My horses were now racing and they were turning out well winning some major two-year-old races. They might prove to be champions over the next five years.

It didn't take long before the two-up game turned savage. A big new player turned up to the game. He was a giant. He was about 35 years old. He introduced himself as Gavin. Some of my staff told me that Gavin was extremely dangerous and had just been released from prison. He'd just finished a 15-year stretch, which had not been for unpaid parking tickets or white-collar crime. He was known to carry a knife and use it on a regular basis. While I was in the room, he showed me total respect and was well-behaved. A few nights later, I had to go out for the night; leaving one of the workers in charge. Gavin asked my worker for some money and was refused. Gavin grabbed some money from the other players, which they'd won themselves and made to leave. My worker yelled out "Stop!" as Gavin was making his exit. In a flash, Gavin had his knife out and had slashed my worker's throat. Blood gushed from his throat. People were screaming as Gavin grabbed more money and calmly walked out informing those present that he'd be back tomorrow for more. Luckily the club was just 200 metres away from the big hospital in Darlinghurst and they saved the life of my worker. I now had some time to worry about Gavin's return.

George Goodman was no help. "Joe, you don't pay me enough for me to get involved. You'll have to sort it out yourself."

I thought about this. Should I just walk away, or should I confront Gavin? People suggested it was only a matter of time before Gavin was arrested and sent back to prison. Maybe Gavin would stay away and the problem would sort itself out. I felt we hadn't seen the last of him. I called Sergei for his advice. He came into the club and talked to me. Sergei knew a mixed martial arts expert who could be hired for the night to help us deal with Gavin. He was available tonight at a cost of $5,000. He came in 30 minutes later. He was a tall man, six foot five inches, and his body was 265 pounds of pure muscle. He had a ponytail and looked a lot like tough guy action-movie star Steven Seagal. I showed him the bloodstained carpet from last night's incident. He was speechless.

"In two hours' time, he'll be coming up those stairs and I need your help to stop him coming in."

Our martial arts expert didn't look at all confident. I showed him my gun, and explained I'd have his back and could use it on Gavin should the situation escalate. Ponytail Seagal saw this was for real and started trembling. Sergei could sense that his man wasn't all he was cracked up to be. Ponytail said he needed to go and get his own gun, for protection and insurance, and would return in half an hour. Sergei assured me that he was good, capable and had guts. We never saw him again. I really needed our Seagal-lookalike to be with us, because we were *Under Siege*.

Two hours later, the welcoming posse was just Sergei and I as Gavin walked up the stairs. I had no option but to confront him myself, "Gavin, stop! I can't let you in tonight."

"Why fucking not?" he wanted to know.

"Gavin, someone nearly died last night; the man whose throat you slashed. At any moment, police could run up here and arrest you. I don't know you that well Gavin, but everyone is terrified of you. Could you please just stay away from this place for a few months?" My tone was respectful but firm. Gavin had showed me respect in our earlier dealings and I needed all of that right now.

Gavin looked me in the eyes, but his expression was cold. I felt this was it for me, Gavin could take me out at any time. "I'm sorry for what happened last night, Joe" he told me. "I'm just out of jail, I've got nothing, I've got nowhere to live, no food, I'm fucked up right now, can you understand that?"

"Let me help you out Gavin. Let me do you a deal." I reached into my jacket slowly and took out five hundred-dollar notes for him; taking care not to show him the other cash I had on me, or my gun. "Take this, Gavin, but this money comes at a price. If ever I'm sent to jail, and you're there and you find me, you look after me in there. Do I make myself perfectly clear?"

Gavin's eyes lit up. He took the money, thanked me, and apologised for what had happened the night before. The way my life was going, with my deeper involvement in the gambling activities of Goodman's mob, jail time might not be too far away. An ally on the inside could certainly be a big help. Gavin apologised again and walked out.

Goodman rang me the next day. He was pleased that everything had worked out. "I'm sorry, Joe. I should have helped you with that guy."

So, after the biggest problem I'd ever faced, I learned one thing. You have to stand up and sort out your own problems. There are a lot of pretenders out there. By sorting out the situation, I earned even more admiration from George. Sergei was amazed that I'd faced Gavin and found a solution when his own man, Ponytail, had turned tail.

I Leave the Underworld

A few months into the new decade of the 1990s, my illegal casino activities came to an end. George Goodman died suddenly. It was a big shock. He was just 55 years old. I didn't go to the funeral, but everyone else did. It was a who's-who of the underworld. A week later, I was encouraged to sell my share of the three racehorses. I valued them at a million dollars, five times the $190,000 we'd bought them for. They were sold at a country auction. An anonymous buyer got them for just $250,000. I got scammed. My return share was $80,000 which was the same as my initial investment. And one of George's old lieutenants wanted a piece of that. I refused to give him anything. Two weeks later my SP club partners wanted to buy me out of the club. I agreed to this. I no longer felt safe or comfortable working with them. A few days later the police raided the two-up game. Nobody had tipped us off. The writing was on the wall. Things were falling apart. The great days of the Sydney casinos were coming to an end.

Journalists were getting nosy and putting two and two together; adding pressure to politicians to clean up the scene. Some of George's men got arrested; something that never happened in the old days.

So far, I wasn't seen as a key member of the underworld. Three of George's partners found themselves in jail soon afterwards for extortion and contempt of court; lying under oath. The net was closing in and if the authorities rounded up the gambling operators and SP bookies, then I could well be calling on Gavin's protection in jail.

The Aussie Mob collapsed, as the old guard were rounded up and arrested. This created a power vacuum in the Cross. The casinos got shut down again. The Gaming and Vice Squad were all put on suspension because many were known to be corrupt. With nothing to do for a while, I took a back seat and watched events unfold. Young Lebanese guys now came into the Cross; claiming that it was their territory. They were much more interested in the lucrative drug trade than in running casinos. With the arrival of this new power into the Cross, the streets of Sydney became more dangerous than ever.

With Sergei's help I started up another poker game. Not a 24x7 club but at least something. Within weeks we had dozens of players. We were the only big game in town. But the Lebanese guys tried to shake me down for too much money and they also borrowed money to gamble at my game without ever intending to pay it back.

After some frustrating months, I had to accept that there was no future dealing with the new guys. They didn't appreciate a well-run gambling club. The clubs these guys were interested in, were strip clubs and brothels. It was street-level, too low-grade for me to be concerned with. There was nothing in the Cross for me anymore. My time in the Sydney underworld was finally over.

RUSSIA

Flight to Russia

I didn't have a lot on my plate at the end of 1992. Sergei came to me to ask if I'd be interested in going to Moscow with him and setting up a casino. I could meet the 10 out of 10 girls there; not those 8 out of 10 girls I had in Sydney. I needed a new challenge. There was nothing going on in the Cross, and Perth had no appeal.

I asked Sergei what I could expect in Moscow. What would be my salary, where would I live, who would pay my expenses and what percentage share would I have in the new casino? Sergei's answers were to my liking. I'd get a salary of $5 000 to $7 000 US a month. I'd have a couple of percentage points in the casino. I'd have luxury accommodation in the centre of Moscow with all my expenses paid. I wouldn't even need to bring any money with me. Everything would be provided for me over there. But bring warm clothing. Very, very, warm clothing. On top of this, I'd be General Manager, and control all the expenses and running of the casino. The casino would be ready to open in three months.

It sounded too good to be true. I thought about it day and night. This opportunity was at the very least worth going over to Russia and investigating. I agreed to make the trip. Sergei asked me to pay for my own airfare (about $3,000) and a travel visa for Russia, another $500. Having been promised rivers of cash at this brand-new casino, I was taken aback at having to fork out a few grand in travel costs. I could easily afford it of course, but people rolling out the red carpet normally let you walk along it free of charge.

Sergei and I caught an Aeroflot plane from Sydney to Moscow; with a stopover for refuelling in Bangkok, Thailand. This was my first ever flight out of Australia. We were joined by four other men. There was a professional Iranian wrestler, who'd won a silver medal at the World Championships. His name was Sayeed. The second addition was a nightclub owner; in fact, the Martial Arts expert who'd run away from Gavin in the Cross days. The Steven Seagal-wannabe. I called him Ponytail. The other two were a big Russian businessman, Leon, and a successful clothing retailer named Alex. I was pleased that our group wasn't just Sergei and me. Now I'd know a few people in Russia upon my arrival.

As we boarded the plane, I was struck with how old it was. The cabin had stained seats, dirty carpet, and such a strong smell of cigarettes, I expected to see lit ones. The airhostesses wore old uniforms which weren't even ironed. They were attractive ladies, but they didn't smile and the coffee they served was not worthy of the name. The food was next-to inedible, salty pickled herring with overripe tomato and hard stale black bread. At least the flight gave us a lot of time to talk. Sergei boasted how we'd all have beautiful women to accompany us and that we'd all learn the Russian language easily.

We'd have a big posse of gangsters to look after us; they'd be meeting us at the airport. Leon told us he had a four-storey office in the commercial centre of Moscow. The first casino in Moscow had just opened and was raking in two to three million US dollars a month. We would be opening Moscow's third casino, and our accommodation was ready to go.

We finally touched down at Moscow's Sheremetyevo International Airport. I've never been so happy to get off a plane in my life. It was over thirty hours since we'd left Sydney and I was starving and tired. It was 8.30 a.m. Moscow time, and it wasn't going to be a warm day. The lines of people waiting to get through customs were at least two hundred metres long. There was a lot of push and shove from passengers trying to get in front; some rough looking people simply walked right to the front of the line. People were screaming abuse at each other.

The airport had been cleaned by the same people who'd cleaned the plane: Nobody. It was old, dirty, and dusty. After 90 minutes of queueing, we finally got our turn at customs. The guards had old uniforms on. They were unshaven and they all chain-smoked. They asked us for our passports and to declare any money we were carrying. Sergei had told me not to bring money on the flight; but I'd ignored that and had over $2,000 US dollars. This was the currency the Russians really loved.

Sergei, Sayeed and Ponytail looked at my money in amazement. After the guards counted it, they wrote numbers onto a long list on some pieces of paper. It took them forever. They then checked me out for non-cash valuables; whether I was wearing any jewellery and what kind of watch I was wearing. Did I want to declare any gold or diamonds? Sayeed and Ponytail were waved through, claiming they'd brought no money with them. This seemed crazy to me. How on earth can you go anywhere and not carry any cash? Alex had a lot of cash on him however, about $5,000 and again it was going to take forever for the Russian customs guys to write numbers onto their lists. The smartest of our crew was Leon. He called the customs manager aside and handed him $300. In return for this obvious bribe, he was waved through with no search conducted and was given a blank signed receipt. He could fill in this receipt himself to say whatever he had in his bag or on his person had been approved by the customs guards.

The Russian Office

At last, we were out of the airport. We were met by Russian eight men. They were our drivers and bag handlers. They would take us to Leon's office. The cars they had were impressive; a black Mercedes Four-Wheel-Drive and black Mercedes SLE sedans. Finally, some class and luxury after the horrible plane, third-rate airport and third-world customs staff. We rode in different cars, each accompanied by two Russian gangsters. It felt powerful to travel this way.

The 4WD drove at the head of our convoy with a blue light flashing and a siren blaring. This looked like it gave our cars the right to drive at any speed and not be stopped by the police for traffic violations. We roared down the highway towards Moscow. Leon had said it would take about eighty minutes to get into town this time of day; our driver said he could do it in fifty.

The vehicles in our convoy drove ten metres apart. The gangster in my car introduced himself to me in broken English, saying his name was Bob. We barrelled along at 80 miles per hour and swerved all over the road. This was to dodge potholes. The ones we drove into sent me crashing into the ceiling even though the suspension on the new Mercedes was pretty good. Whenever the driving got really hairy, Bob turned back to look at me, to judge how much fear I was experiencing. Once we neared the city proper, we couldn't speed anymore and about ten miles out of Moscow, we were now slow and safe enough that I could let go of the hang-your-coat-here handle above the back door.

We were now stuck in heavy traffic and couldn't move. The 4WD put the siren on again and veered off the road and straight onto the big wide footpath. Pedestrians jumped out of the way as we drove for three hundred metres on the footpath. I'd never seen this before, not even in the movies. I saw traffic police respecting our siren and leaving us alone. We returned to the road, cutting off another driver who blared his horn and extended his middle finger to us.

This provocation was too much for the gangsters in our convoy to ignore. Five of them got out of our convoy's cars, armed with baseball bats. They ran towards the upset driver who'd flipped them the bird. They dragged him out of his car, punched him up a bit, but as a special favour to him, they didn't use the baseball bats. The driver thanked the Russian mafia guys for giving him another chance. This was a show of strength from the mobsters for the benefit of us Aussies. If it wasn't for us, I think the mafia guys would've left the driver alone.

We got to Leon's office without further pavement driving or intimidation. The office was a mafia stronghold. We drove under a high archway into another courtyard and parked next to more black Mercedes sedans. Two young guys with AK47 Kalashnikov rifles guarded the vehicles for us. The cars had to be watched continuously. Other gangs tried to take out members of our gang by attaching car explosives to unattended vehicles. This was our mob's stronghold, where they could defend themselves and perhaps the only place in all of Russia where they could sleep safely at night.

When we got inside the building, we were scanned with metal detectors, to check that we weren't armed. We were taken to a small cafeteria inside and offered tea and coffee. The cafe had an Italian Espresso machine, one of just three in Moscow at the time. Sergei said he had something to show me and took me down into the cellar of the building. The cellar smelled like an open toilet. Once my eyes got used to the dark, I saw that it was a small private jail! There were four cells and a guard with the keys to each cell. One guy was imprisoned, the three other cells were empty. The prisoner owed money to the mafia. As soon as his family paid up and settled his debt, he'd be released.

The Russian mob were impressing me with their methods so far. We had a meeting in their conference room; sitting at long parallel tables while the top guys in the organisation sat at a small head table. Waiters came around pouring vodka into small glasses and orange juice into larger vessels. One of the top bosses said something in Russian and the bosses raised their vodka glasses then sculled the strong liquor in one hit, followed by orange juice at the usual speed. It was vodka and orange, in that order. Food was then served; cheese, salami, smoked salmon and bread. The salmon was a disappointment. I was used to much better in Sydney. But I was that hungry, that I ate it. Everyone proceeded to make a toast.

The locals got jollier and jollier, but I got more and more frustrated at this meaningless get together. I don't know if it was the jet lag, but it seemed to me that this went on for at least seven hours. Maybe they would dull our senses with all these vodka toasts, and we'd be marched to their basement prison and kept until our families paid some hitherto-unknown debt to them. This would take kidnap and ransom to international levels.

A Luxury Apartment

At last, we were released. It was time to go to our luxury apartment. On the way to our accommodation, Sergei pointed out the main stadium used in the 1980 Moscow Olympics. He said we were in the Olimpisky Prospekt and close to our apartment. Opposite the stadium was the Penta hotel, a German-run five-star hotel used by international visitors to the city. I guessed that our apartments had been built as athletes' accommodation just over ten years earlier and had since been converted to quality apartments.

Our apartment was just behind the Penta. It was in an eight story building of dull architecture and there were no lights on in the building as we drove up. We parked the cars near the reception office and stepped out into an inch of mud. There was no concrete or bitumen in the carpark.

The building was damp, cold, and dirty. It looked forty years old. If this had been the athletes' accommodation for the 1980 Olympics, no wonder the US had boycotted the Games! The Soviet invasion of Afghanistan had just been an excuse, the Americans actually pulled out so they wouldn't have to stay in this shithole.

We were met by a woman with a kerosene lamp and a torch. She warmed her hands close to the lamp. We introduced ourselves and told her our apartment number. She found the keys for us in her office; which also had her sleeping bed in it and an ancient telephone.

She showed us where the elevator shaft was. As the elevator was coming down to meet us, she yelled a warning to Sergei in

Russian. Sergei translated for us. The floor of the elevator was unsafe. We had to look carefully where we were standing. We waited five minutes for the elevator to reach the ground floor. Once inside, Sergei lit a match so we could see the floor. It was made of thin particleboard and there was a huge crack on the back right corner. You could easily fall through it to your death. I told Sergei this was crazy and that people could die, falling right through the crack in the corner. He said no, not really, everyone knew about the problem and there had not been an incident in two years.

"Two years?" I asked. "If it had been a problem for two years, why hadn't they fixed it?" Simple. Nobody wanted to spend the money.

The apartments looked small. I asked Sergei how many rooms ours had. He said two. Two rooms for four adult men. We got to our apartment and Sergei rang a doorbell. We were let in by a young Russian lady; who took a few minutes to unbolt four locks from the inside and glare at us through a peephole. It was starting to look like we were in a really bad area. There was actually a second door to pass through to get into the apartment proper; it was like an airlock or a bank vault. This two-door arrangement was to keep the heat in and the thieves out.

Our bags filled the kitchen. The water system in the toilet was leaky, noisy, and broken. Just walking around made the old carpet filthier. I knew right away that I couldn't sleep here. There was only one bedroom.

"Two rooms, Sergei?" I asked him.

"Of course Joe; one bedroom, one living room. That's two rooms."

"I haven't come halfway across the world to live like this."

"What can I do, Joe? This is Russia."

The Russian girl, Anna, was stunning. She was a blue-eyed blonde in her twenties. Sergei kissed her as our drivers and bag handlers left. I knew Sergei was not originally from Moscow. He'd left Russia for Israel before ending up in Sydney. I asked him how he knew the girl. He replied that she'd been hired by the Mob as a cleaner and bed-warmer for $200 a month plus free accommodation; great money in Moscow where $90 a month was an average wage. I just wanted to get out of this horrible place.

None of us had showered for 48 hours and the bathroom here wasn't the place to do it. I changed into a track suit and was given a pillow and a thin blanket. I laid down on the couch. The others were jealous of my prime sleeping arrangements. Sayeed said he would sleep in the entrance hall. Sergei and Anna were already in bed together.

Sayeed cried out that there was water on the floor in the hall. Sergei called out to come into the bedroom and sleep on the floor there. Anna complained about this, but Sergei said something in Russian and it sounded threatening. Sayeed went into the room. A few minutes later we heard the bed squeaking and slapping sounds. "Keep going you bitch," Sergei said. He was fucking Anna with Sayeed two feet away. The rest of us giggled. We knew what was happening in the bedroom.

Sergei was a totally different man in Russia than he had been in Sydney. I'd never seen him like this before. He treated Anna like shit and enjoyed degrading her in front of Sayeed. I'd been in Russia for just one day and it was nothing like what I'd expected. Sergei had sold me on the idea of luxury and glamour. This was tawdry and cheap.

I managed to get a few hours of sleep and in the morning it was time to use the toilet. The stench was unbearable, but I had to sit and shit. Everyone in the apartment could hear the noises I was making, despite my attempts to be silent. Once I finished, I saw there was no toilet paper; just a stack of cut-up newspaper. I guess that functioned as toilet paper in Russia. Christ, what must life have been like under the Soviets a few years ago if Russia was now the modern land of opportunity? Sitting on the toilet, it was clear I couldn't endure these conditions for more than two days and I'd have to move to the Penta hotel nearby. "Fuck you, Sergei, there's no way all of us can live in this shit apartment," I told him outside.

"Joe, be reasonable. In Moscow, this is considered a VIP apartment, it's costing me $500 a month. This isn't room 1415 at the Sydney Hilton. You're in Russia now."

"Yeah, I'm in Russia but I'm not staying here. I'll go and stay in the Penta."

"The Penta will cost you four hundred US dollars a night. You can stay there five days with that two thousand you brought with you."

Sergei didn't know that I always believe in having a Plan B. My health and safety will never be at risk to any gang or anybody. Sayeed and Ponytail were happy that I was leaving; more space for them. The prime sleeping area of the couch was now up for grabs. I wheeled out my heavy suitcase; remembering to avoid death corner in the elevator. It was nine in the morning and freezing cold. Just getting to the Penta hotel was going to be a dangerous experience.

The Penta Hotel

I made it to the Penta. It took me half an hour to get there, dragging my heavy suitcase. I'd only slept three hours in the last seventy-two. When I got to reception I asked to speak to the manager, to negotiate a room rate for a long stay. I had to wait fifteen minutes to see him.

The manager was a middle-aged Englishman, pleased to talk to someone with native English who wouldn't give him trouble. He picked my accent as Australian and met my price of $250 a night for a month. I left him my whole $2,000 as the deposit and they had a room ready for me right away, I wouldn't have to wait until 1 p.m. They took my bags, and I followed my porter to my room. Once the porter left me alone, I continued with my implementation of Plan B. I took out my old sports jacket and started unpicking the seams on the shoulders. I'd sewn $5,000 in each shoulder. This undeclared money would come in very handy until the casino was up and running and money was flowing from that source.

I then took out the rest of my clothes and settled into the room. Finally, I took a shower, my first in days. I used a whole bottle of body-wash to get thoroughly clean. After drying myself, I went straight to bed, climbing between those sweet smelling clean sheets. I'd survived the first day.

I woke up nine hours later, refreshed and hungry again. A message light was flashing on my phone. I asked the concierge to bring me my message and ordered a room service meal; veal schnitzel with salad and fries and some coffee. It was now 7pm, still very bright outside. The message said "Everyone will be in the office at 9 p.m. Very important. Be there." Five minutes after the message, my food arrived. The most beautiful girl I'd ever laid eyes on brought in a tray with my meal and coffee on it.

I couldn't help check her out as she bent over and placed the food on my table. She had a magnificent body. Surely, she was a ten on the Sergei scale. She asked in excellent English if I'd like anything else.

"Yeah, I'd like something else, but I can't tell you what that is right now," I teased her. I signed the cheque and she walked out, knowing that I was still enjoying the shape of her body.

I dressed for the trip to the office and put on aftershave. I went down to the hotel lobby to organise a ride to the office. The hotel's town car would cost $25, very expensive for a short ride. I would need to figure out cheaper transport sooner or later, I might as well start tonight. A receptionist suggested I flag down a black Volga, a Russian taxi, and show them the office address. She wrote it down for me in Russian. She gave me a card with the hotel's name and address in Russian for the return trip. She also changed a US $100 note for me and got me some Russian roubles.

The receptionist was capable and friendly. I asked her if every girl in Moscow was as friendly as she was. She replied probably not, but I was the hotel's first Australia guest and she'd heard from her colleague how handsome I was.

"You mean the room service girl?"

"Yes, that's her, she said very nice things about you."

Things were looking up at the Penta.

Getting My Share

Within a minute of stepping out onto the street, I hailed a black Volga and arranged for the drive to the office. I gave the driver the paper with the address on it and two US dollars. He encouraged me to sit with him in the front. The Volgas were Russian-made cars, very cheap and hard working, they reminded me of the Australian HR Holdens from the 1970s. The driver was a chain smoker, spilling ash everywhere in his car. He took me to the entrance of my mob office. I walked through the archway into the courtyard. A new young guy with a Kalashnikov motioned his gun at me and made sure I waited until he checked I had proper business there.

A giant mobster came out and told the gun-toting guard that I was OK. The giant took me up to the conference room. This wasn't a vodka and orange toasting day; this was serious business. The five people in my group were arranging business with the Mob's main man, St. Petersburg Bob. The huge guy who fetched me from the courtyard was his second in command, let's call him Wardrobe. The other three guys on the mob side were all brothers and all veteran hit men who had each killed more than once. The final mobster was a young man named Marek, who spoke excellent English and translated for us. Marek had known St. Petersburg Bob in jail and had got on so well with him that he joined the gang once he was released.

SP Bob spoke for five minutes in Russian then Sergei repeated in English for our benefit. We'd come here to set up a casino, restaurant and nightclub. The managers would be me and

Ponytail Seagal. Alex would open six clothing stores in the retail centre of Moscow at a 70/30 split for him; a few years down the track it would be 50/50. Alex would finance the stores and the casino at a total investment of two million US dollars. Sayeed would help Ponytail and me with security, and would also be used by the Russian mob for muscle jobs.

The casino would be managed by our group on a 15 percent management agreement. Investors would get another 45 percent and our group would get the remaining 40 percent. There was no investment needed from our side. Bob wanted Ponytail and me to go and see the site tomorrow, but I wasn't happy with the proposed money split.

"What will my percentage of the casino be, Bob?"

"As far as I know Joe, you're getting a good salary and if your bosses want to give you a piece from the 15 percent management fee, that's up to Sergei and Leon."

"I've never worked for a salary in my life. I have also never co-managed any casino."

Sergei and Leon laughed loudly at this. I was in Russia now and I'd have to do things their way. "You won't be able to do anything without us, Joe," Sergei explained. "Do you know, ten foreigners have already died trying to set up casinos here."

"Well that's interesting, but this is a completely different story to what you told me in Sydney. I was never told that we'd just be management."

"Joe, you came here as part of a group," Bob reminded me, even though I'd only met the rest of my group on the plane over. "They got you your tickets, your visa, your accommodation."

"The fuck they got me tickets, visa and accommodation! I paid for my own flight and my own visa. The accommodation was way below standard, and I've already moved out."

This was news to SP Bob. As Marek translated, he watched Sergei closely, looking for confirmation or denial of my claims. There was an animated chat in Russian between the three of them.

"Joe, if you work for us, you'll make three times what you did in Australia. How much did you make last year?"

"Over a million dollars," I told him.

"Bullshit. Why would you leave Australia and come here, if you were already making over a million?"

"I'm here to make millions and millions more. I'm not just a casino manager. I am a professional gambler. I have many talents and I am going to make first millions, and then tens of millions." I said.

"You're a gambler, Joe?" confirmed St Petersburg Bob.

"I'm a professional in most forms of gambling. I succeed where others fail. I'm unique, flexible and I can adapt to any environment, provided I can implement my own ideas without interference."

SP Bob and Wardrobe were impressed with my spiel. The talents I was describing were respected in the Russian underworld.

"Well Joe, come all this way, please don't got upset with us. Please come and have a look at the operation we're setting up. Take a look at the other two casinos already here and have a look at the one we're building. There's plenty of money around for everyone."

"Sure, I'll stay for a month. It'll cost me about $10,000 in expenses but I'm happy to do that. I think that Russia is a very interesting place. I'm interested in seeing how Russian people think. Not to mention the Russian girls."

"Joe, we need a lot of girls," Marek said. "In fact, we'll need over eighty girls working. Dealers, receptionists, waitresses. You can choose any ladies you want. Hire and train them yourself."

This was a great idea. I thought about Anna in that horrible apartment and what she'd done with Sergei. All for $200 a month. Smiling, I agreed to Marek's proposal. But there was still the matter of my expenses; the casino was still a few months away from opening.

Leon explained that there wasn't a sea of money yet, "Joe, six weeks ago, Sergei's lawyer jumped out of a tenth story window and killed himself. Sergei is broke now; he's desperate and completely broke. All he has now is you and this casino deal."

Many businessmen kept their money with accountants and lawyers, in tax-minimisation schemes that hid their money from the taxman. Sergei had the great misfortune of choosing the wrong man to manage his money. He and many others had been swindled out of their money by a cheat who had taken the easy way out as the net was closing in on him.

This explained why Sergei fucked Anna in the apartment in front of Sayeed. It was the animal act of a man with nothing to lose.

"I'm not a commodity," I pointed out. "Nobody owns me, I'm not a slave."

Sergei piped up, "Joe, I helped you out from the start, I lent you $40,000 in Sydney to get your first casino up and going."

It was a drop in the ocean for him years ago. Now he was desert dry.

"Sergei, you lent me $40,000 and I repaid you with full interest and a few more weeks of bonus payments. We were square long ago. I owe you nothing. We've had some great times together, but you should have told me the truth before I came to Russia. This is Bait-and-Switch."

Marek tried to smooth things over, "Stop arguing, let's start making money. Joe, I'll take you and Sergei to the two casinos that are already operating. That'll give you an idea of the standard of our competition. Take some notes of what you see Joe. What works and what doesn't. See what we'll need in our casino. At 7 p.m. we'll go for dinner at our restaurant and then I'll show you our casino building."

I went back to my hotel in shock. Sergei's news was devastating. He was broke, mentally deranged, unhinged. I had already noticed he hadn't been himself recently. I put it down to nerves about the big Russian trip; but now I knew there was much more to it than that. The success of this venture was do or die for him.

I patted myself on the back about my Plan B. My emergency money was being put to the best possible use; keeping me secure in the hotel and away from that god-awful apartment. $10,000 US was a lot of money in Moscow in 1993. The other four people who'd come to Russia with me were broke, desperate and dangerous. I wondered how long my money would last me. Maybe only two months.

Gabriella's Casino

It was now time for our first casino visit. It was called Gabriella's Casino and was open twenty-four seven. It was owned by a wealthy ex-KGB guy who named the casino after his daughter. He also had Gabriella's Casinos in St. Petersburg and Kiev. His casinos were making him even wealthier.

We drove right into the centre of Moscow; fifty metres away was Red Square where the Kremlin is and where they have the famous military parades. I'd seen them many times on TV. We parked in front of the Intourist hotel, which had the usual carpark full of black Mercedes, each with a driver waiting. This was a classic two or three star Soviet-era hotel. Functional but with no luxury.

Security waved metal-detector wands over us to check that we were unarmed. We were eyed off in the lobby by twenty prostitutes. They weren't top-class. They looked like single mothers from the country towns outside Moscow. They were smoking and plainly dressed like shop assistants. The world's oldest profession is often seen at casinos, but the ladies are normally better presented than this. The going rate was $100 US for two hours upstairs.

There was another metal detector check going onto the gaming floor, and they also photocopied our passport ID page. We weren't allowed to bring our coats onto the floor; we had to surrender them to a cloak room. We were given numbered tickets to redeem our coats on the way out. Luckily, the casino was well heated. This was one part of Moscow where we wouldn't freeze without our coats on.

The gaming floor was basically a converted conference room. There were ten tables, a bar, the cloak room, and the staff entrance. On the other side were some management offices and the cashier. The decor was blue velvet. It reminded me of a casino in London. The casino equipment they used was from John Huxley, a London company. Very good quality. The one problem with the casino was the carpet. It was cheap and hadn't been properly cleaned for a long time.

It was 2 p.m., normally a quiet time in a casino, but things were quite busy. Looking around I noticed some different groups of people playing, all of them gangsters from different groups. There were Chechens, Armenians, Georgians, and some Russians.

So, this whole casino was a mafia hang-out. Everyone was playing in US dollars which impressed me. The customers had money. Watching some blackjack players, I saw they had no idea about the game. Not just the players but the management too. The casino had only been open two months. Watching the money take at the tables, I estimated that the casino would make about US $200,000 a day, way more than I'd expected.

The security at the blackjack tables was dreadful. On several occasions a player facing a decision to hit or stand waited while his gangster friend peeped at the next card in the deck and gave him perfect advice! Also, there was a surrender option available when the dealer showed an ace. The players I saw were so bad that one hit to make 18, the other players stood, and the dealer with an ace showing duly completed blackjack against the idiots who had refused to surrender.

The English manager of the club confirmed that surrendering to a dealer's ace was possible in this casino and added that the players were so bad that the casino got all their money soon enough anyhow. Bingo. I'd found an absolute money tree. I could win a fortune playing blackjack here, even without card counting. Somehow the dealers here, many of them ex-London, knew nothing about running blackjack properly and the managers were just as clueless.

I sat down to play. I won $2,500 in less than an hour and quit, the game was just too easy. I didn't want to draw too much attention to myself. This was a game I could return to again and again. Sayeed, Sergei and Ponytail didn't see how much money I could make by playing at this goldmine.

Sergei suggested we all go out and eat at a Georgian restaurant he knew. I cashed in and tried hiding my excitement from the others in my group. The barman chased us for our drinks bill. The bill was excessive; $4 US for a coffee, $6,50 for a mineral water. This casino was making big money from the drinks too. I guess since they gave away thousands of dollars to anyone who understood blackjack, they deserved to sell overpriced drinks in return. I paid $40 for our table's bill and needed a bathroom visit before we left.

Christ. The toilets were dreadful. Just like the apartment from hell that I'd escaped. They didn't have toilet paper. Cut newspaper was provided for arse-wiping. There was no soap and nothing to dry your hands with. I couldn't believe that a casino taking $200,000 and up a day couldn't do better for their bathrooms. No wonder the place was just a mob hangout and there were few foreigners or businessmen playing. No wonder there were no women on the gaming floor. In fact, the only women I'd seen were the casino staff and the prostitutes in the lobby.

A Georgian Meal

The Georgian restaurant had something memorable at its entrance. A giant stuffed black bear! Sergei asked me if I had troubles to pay for the dinner. I only had US dollars. Sergei took $200 from me to change into roubles, telling me to order whatever food I liked, it was very cheap here. The rest of us couldn't read the menu; it was all Russian. The numbers on the menu were certainly low, everything was two or three roubles. We ordered some coal-roasted chicken and pork shashliks in spicy Georgian sauce. Shashliks are grilled skewers of meat, some cultures call them shish kebabs. Five of us were at a table that could seat twelve people.

I ordered ten pork and ten chicken shashliks, and ten breads on the side. Sayeed, a Muslim, wouldn't touch pork so he asked for soup with lamb meat balls; I ordered six of those too. Sayeed told me that Sergei hadn't been feeding him well; and that life in the apartment was just as bad as I remembered.

Sergei was back twenty minutes later with the roubles and two of the Russian gang, Wardrobe and the young guy who minded the Kalashnikovs in the boot of the car. There was plenty of room for the new arrivals. It was just as well that I'd ordered plenty of food. Five minutes later, Marek joined us. He talked closely with Sergei and they were both looked at me regularly. Things got down to business soon enough. Sergei sidled up to me.

"Joe, we need to talk. How much did you win at blackjack today?"

"Just over twenty-five hundred. $2,575 to be exact."

"Well played. You know Joe, any money you make in Moscow has to be shared; 20% for Wardrobe and Marek, 40% for me and Leon."

Gambling winnings are sometimes split, but only with backers, the people who put up the money to gamble with in the first place. I was gambling entirely with my own money and Sergei and nobody else had any claim to any share of my winnings. I couldn't help noticing that the other two international visitors, Ponytail and Sayeed, were left out of Sergei's proposed percentage split.

"Hang on, this has got nothing to do with you. What does my gambling have to do with you or Leon? Or with Wardrobe and Marek?"

"I brought you here, Joe, and Wardrobe and Marek are protecting you. You're in Russia now, Joe, don't forget. This isn't Sydney anymore."

I shook my head and rolled my eyes. How much does a share of $2,575 mean to a big Mafia group? I knew Sergei really needed whatever money he could get his hands on and wanted to show off his worth to the Russian Mob. I was still mulling over what to do with my winnings when the food arrived.

The food was great, and we wolfed it down. Wardrobe, who was a very large Russian, ate three plates of shashlik in ten minutes. His body size was no accident. Sayeed ate three chicken shashliks. I then ordered vodka, cognac and orange juice. We ate and drank like Tsars for three hours. It came time for me to do the money split of the $2,500 winnings.

I pulled out $900 and gave Wardrobe $300 and Sergei $600. Wardrobe pocketed his cash with a smile, for Sergei it wasn't enough.

"Joe that's wrong, it's 20% for Wardrobe and 40% for me. 40% of $2,500 is $1,000."

"You know, Sergei, who is paying my expenses? Oh, I remember now - me. It's costing me $300 a day for me to live here; hotel, food, women. I'm taking that off the top before we split the rest. Today's adjusted winnings are $1,500. 40% for you is $600, 20% for Wardrobe is $300. Take it or leave it."

Sergei had become a cheap cunning rat. He warned me that he'd better get his full share. The bill arrived and I asked him for the roubles. He gave me my $200 worth. The bill for the whole night was the equivalent of $80; amazingly cheap for dinner and drinks for eight people. At these prices I could have fed the bear at the entrance.

Sayeed looked upset.

"You're not still hungry surely, Sayeed?"

"No, Joe, but I don't have money for coffee and food tomorrow."

I gave him $100 dollars and some roubles. Seeing this, Sergei gave the same amount to Ponytail.

Wardrobe nodded his head in approval at how Sergei and I looked after the other guys in our team. He saw me as a generous person. I told everyone that I needed to go back to my hotel, rest for a while, then I'd inspect the other casino later.

The following week Sayeed, Ponytail and I had a second Georgian meal. Just the three of us, without Sergei or our Russian gangsters. The restaurant charged us $230 for our $23 meal.

"None of you are Russians," they explained; the small prices on the menu only applied to locals. Russians, of all ages and occupations, were tireless in their efforts to cheat foreigners.

A Hot Dog in Red Square

Red Square. I felt like a tourist as I walked around it before my next visit to Gabriella's. Tonight, it was pretty quiet. There were around a hundred tourists and ten police. There were no food shops or souvenir shops, though I did see a most American food option - a hot dog stand.

The hot dog's price was exorbitant - a full US five dollars. Obviously, this was a price for tourists, but still, if tourists to Red Square were paying this much for a hot dog the guy was doing very well. As I left I saw a gangster approaching the stand for his cut of the profits. Another tourist bus pulled up and ten tourists got out, some going to the hot dog stand. This was a good business. The seller was protected by a mob and the police were leaving him alone. They were probably getting a share of the action as well.

At Gabriella's that night, it wasn't all gangsters. There was a group of fifteen to twenty mainland Chinese playing, and like a lot of Chinese, they loved gambling.

The Chinese were great customers. Looking around I saw the usual mafia gangs, but I also heard two Americans speaking with New York accents. I introduced myself and got to chatting with them. They were immigrants to Russia, like Sergei and Leon. We spoke about the gambling scene in Moscow; they told me about a casino poker game they knew of. This was music to my ears, so I left to check this game out. The mafia guys watched me leave. They were interested that I'd come to the casino, stayed for just a short time, chatted to the Americans and left right after. I hailed a Volga and told the driver to take me to the Hippodrome Royal Casino.

Poker at the Royal

The Royal casino was the most beautiful building of any casino I'd ever seen. It was next to a horseracing track and had previously been the member's enclosure. It had since been renovated at a cost of millions of dollars and now functioned as a casino. This beautiful building would not have looked out of place in Vienna or Monte Carlo. This was a classy place and it didn't have groups of gangsters inside. The staff and security were well-dressed and alert. There was the usual metal-detector wand and passport check at the lobby. Going into the casino was like going into a palace. There were carved statues, marble columns, and high painted and engraved ceilings.

There was a poker table at the back, which was managed by a Singaporean-Chinese guy, Sam, who had casino experience across Europe. The poker table was full of players. The rest of the casino was about half full. I saw two players betting big at their own private table. They were betting $1,000 a number on roulette. Approaching the poker table, I was told that if I wanted to play, I needed to talk to Chinese Sam.

There was only one Chinese guy in the management, so I knew who to ask. "Good evening. I'd like to play poker tonight please. Is there a waiting list I can join?"

"Good evening to you, sir. My name's Sam. May I ask where you're from?"

"Nice to meet you, Sam. I'm Joe, I'm from Sydney, Australia."

"Thanks for coming to the Royal Joe, it's a pleasure to meet you too. You've come a long way to be here. What brings you to Moscow?"

Of course I wasn't going to tell him I was here to set up a rival casino. "I'm in the mining business. I'm setting up a sale of some equipment to some interests here." I knew enough about mining that I could bluff my way through any questions that Sam would throw at me.

"That must be big business, Joe. Australia is a big mining country; gold, uranium, iron-ore and coal."

"All of that and more. Aluminium, too." Some of the new Russian millionaires were getting rich from oil and aluminium; Sam would know that. "So, I'll be in Moscow for at least a few months and I like to play poker. Can I get a game here?"

"As you can see, we're full tonight and none of the players will be leaving soon. But if you come tomorrow by 8:50 p.m. I can get you a seat. The game starts at 9 p.m. I run a tight ship here, Joe. I don't allow gangsters or professional players in my game. This is a game for businessmen like yourself."

"That's great, I look forward to playing. I'll see you tomorrow."

This was an excellent development. Finally, a properly fitted-out casino. Their bathroom had proper toilet paper and a hand dryer. Nobody knew me as a poker professional and "Mining Joe" could do very well indeed at this game over the next few weeks. I could hardly wait for tomorrow night. Surely there wouldn't be good poker players in this city of amateurs, who couldn't even play a basic blackjack strategy.

Real Room Service

The two New Yorkers had given me a second tip: go to a bar called Night Flight. It had the most beautiful girls and was open until 4 a.m. It had just opened and was already the place to be for people who liked luxury and a great night out. The New Yorkers proved just as good with this tip as they had with the Hippodrome Royal poker game tip. I had a meeting at 6 p.m. the next day but a few hours at Night Flight were called for.

I had a strong worry that I couldn't shake off. On our first day in Moscow, our mob had taken our passports from us and returned them without the exit visa card in them. This card, unforgeable and covered in official stamps and signatures, was required to leave the country. The exit visas for Sayeed, Ponytail, Leon and I were all being kept in the mob's safe, for "safekeeping". We would be unable to fly out of Russia until we got our exit visas back. We had our passports, we used them for ID to get into the casinos, but just the passports alone were not enough for us to leave Russia. I would think about this a lot more tomorrow, for now it was time to unwind at the nightclub.

The Night Flight was just as good as the Americans had promised. There were eighty stunning girls there and just five men. Good odds in anyone's language. Two girls caught my eye right away and I walked over to them and offered to buy them a drink. As I sipped my Jack Daniels and Coke, talk with the girls soon turned to business. I wanted to take my favourite back to the hotel for a few hours; the girls preferred working as a team.

"Which hotel are you staying at?"

"I'm at the Penta." The girls liked this. Someone staying at the Penta was a man of wealth and taste.

"Oooh that's nice. OK, $150 or, if you like, $250 for the both of us."

"That's tempting, but surely I can only handle one of you, the second would be a waste, right?"

"No no no! We do some very interesting things together. Come on, the three of us together, it'll be great."

"Sold. Let's see what you girls can do."

At the hotel, the girls had to show identification to reception, which they were able to do to their satisfaction. In the room, the girls immediately made their way to the bathroom and I ordered a bottle of champagne and three glasses.

Ten minutes later there was a knock on the door and I opened it to see my favourite room service girl, with the champagne, the three glasses and a complimentary fruit plate. I hadn't shut the bathroom door, and the room service beauty could see the two naked girls towelling each other off in the bathroom. I was embarrassed that she saw those two girls. Had I known it was her bringing the champagne, I would have closed the bathroom door.

To my surprise she didn't disapprove of my party at all. She gave me a dazzling smile and said, "Enjoy the champagne." I certainly did enjoy the champagne that night.

Two nights later in the hotel I was alone, a quiet night with no Night Flight girls. I ordered a room service burger and chips. The same woman brought the meal, and as always, I let her into the room to put down the food from the tray.

"Oh Joe… you're on your own tonight?" She seemed like she wanted to do something about that.

"Yes, just me tonight."

She put her hand on my chest and pushed me against the wall. Her other hand pushed the door shut and locked it. Both hands began exploring my body and soon my trousers were off as she knelt in front of me.

They really look after their guests at the Penta Hotel. This was real room service.

I Can Do This on My Own

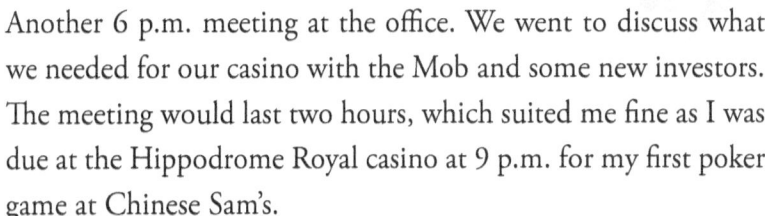

Another 6 p.m. meeting at the office. We went to discuss what we needed for our casino with the Mob and some new investors. The meeting would last two hours, which suited me fine as I was due at the Hippodrome Royal casino at 9 p.m. for my first poker game at Chinese Sam's.

I kicked off the discussion with my report on Gabriella's. They were badly managed, and I could easily do better. Ponytail, who shouldn't even have been at this meeting, burst out laughing and wanted to show he was a bigshot in the Aussie group.

"That's ridiculous, Joe. Gabriella's Casino is making over eight million dollars a month. How do you think you could do better than that? They've got English management, with way more experience than you."

Cheers for that, Ponytail. What a great way of making me look good in front of the investors. Why don't you go home and fetch your gun and not come back again, same as what you did in Kings Cross that night? "Let me tell you what I saw in Gabriella's. The managers are all ex-dealers, who dealt in London casinos a year ago. The gangs are running rampant in the place; the Russian high rollers are too scared to go near the place. When other casinos start up, properly run and with gangsters kept out, Gabriella's will go broke and have no business."

Leon liked my analysis, "But what about the Royal?"

"The Royal is better fitted out and has a better clientele. But the management is old and lazy and not in tune with what Russians want. They feel like they've got enough players as it is, and they're not trying to grow their business. That's a bad attitude."

"So you're confident you can do a better job than both Gabriella's and the Royal?" Leon asked.

"Absolutely. I'm confident, right now, that if I'm put in charge, we will be very successful."

Ponytail couldn't leave me alone. "No, Joe, we're doing this in a corporate manner. We're a business and we'll run it like one. We have meetings and we decide on these things collectively. You're not running this show by yourself."

"That would be a mistake, Ponytail. Look, set some targets for management. I can get the place earning say three million a month for the first four months, and then four to five million per month for the next eight months after that. If I'm not close to those amounts, sack me and get someone else to manage the casino."

The Russian investors were impressed by my high estimates. They'd been expecting a take of one million per month.

Now it was Sergei's turn to say stupid shit, "So did you play in the Royal last night, Joe?"

"My playing is entirely my business, Sergei. What I win or lose is small fry in the big picture of things here."

"No Joe, we have an arrangement here, we're due our share."

"I actually didn't play last night, Sergei, but I'm playing tonight at the Royal at 9 p.m. But, it's a no-pros game, they think I'm in Moscow for a mining deal. If they figure out I'm a pro, or worse still, that I'm in Moscow to set up a rival casino, they'll ban me from the game and the casino.

"Bullshit. You just don't want us to see how much you're making. You're going to rob us of our share."

"That's not true, Sergei. It's a businessman's game, no pros, no gangsters."

"Well we might just check that out for ourselves, Joe." Sergei warned.

"Sergei, that's not a good idea. I spoke to the poker manager yesterday and he warned me that it was a no-pros game. I can do this on my own. If three other guys turn up with Australian passports, they'll know we're connected, and they'll stop me playing there. Trust me, I can make good money in this game, and you'll get your fair share of the winnings."

"Of course we'll leave you alone. We'll watch from a distance. We won't say one word to you. We were going to check out the Royal ourselves tonight anyway."

The next item of business was the clothes shops. I thought that the merchandise was pretty good and that it would sell well in Moscow. Sergei reported that while the shops were doing well, they wouldn't bring in good profit for at least a year. We needed money right now, not down the track. Quick cash right now is what's important. Sergei and the rest of the party were really desperate for money and desperate people do desperate things. The Russian investors could easily be put off by their behaviour.

I had to excuse myself at 8.30 p.m. "OK Gentlemen, I'm off to work, going to the Royal to play poker. Please don't go there tonight, and if you really must, don't hang around me or make any trouble. This should be a good place for me, somewhere I can make some good money."

Poker Interrupted

I got to the casino at 8:45 p.m. The poker table was full but Sam had saved me a seat. Tonight's game had a $2,000 buy-in. This suited me as my cash reserves were $12,000 and a bigger game would have been beyond me. I won a big pot on the first hand and was up $1,500 in less than five minutes. The game continued to be good and by 11 p.m., after two hours play, I was $6,500 to the good. The game was even better than I'd hoped for.

As always in my life, when things are at their best, associates come in and fuck it all up. Ponytail, Sergei, and Leon walked into the casino and they weren't hiding their presence. Ponytail started playing roulette and lost quickly and loudly. He swore at the dealers and drew a lot of attention to himself. He told anyone who would listen what a badly run place this was. Soon after, I noticed Sergei and Leon were behind me. They asked me how much I was in for and how much I was winning. The morons. They'd paid no attention to my instructions to leave me alone and remain inconspicuous.

Chinese Sam saw what was going on in a flash. He'd heard, through the casino grapevine, that Australians were in Moscow to set up a rival casino. He put two and two together and the only answer could be four. Sergei and Leon wandered off, but Sam had seen enough. Nothing was said to me, and the poker game continued on as before, but I had a strong sense that this would be my one and only game at the Royal.

After another hour, at midnight, I was $6,750 up. Chinese Sam was looking at me frequently and I sensed I'd be made to leave soon. He'd seen me with the other Aussies, and could see from my poker play that I knew a lot more about the game than a mining operator. I cashed out, but nobody wished me good luck or said goodbye. I was given the cold shoulder.

The Novy Arbat

We'd now been in Russia for so long that a third casino had opened. The newest casino was on the Novy Arbat, a major Moscow street. This casino was licensed to play using Russian roubles only. Just on that basis alone, I expected it to be the smallest of the casinos that were up and running. I went to check it out.

The casino had a Scottish man as the manager with a Croatian as his offsider. Their names were Gordon and Branco, and they were fun guys. I hit it off with them straight away. They enjoyed Russian women and the fast life of Moscow as much as I did. We shared a few stories of our experiences. There was a poker game going in the back corner. They led me to the game. It was a lot smaller than Chinese Sam's game at the Royal, but it looked like an easy game.

I told my new friends that I'd come back tomorrow and play poker. I didn't have many roubles on me. The casino offered an exchange rate where US $1,000 got you 110,000 roubles. This was downright theft. I could easily get 125,000 roubles on the street. Tomorrow I'd change US $4,000 into roubles, at proper rates, and play in this new poker game.

The next day, after a full eight hours sleep, I hit the streets to get money changed, I was prepared to bargain with different money changers and get the best price I could. I had the time to do this. I saw some amazing things on the streets. I saw an Armenian man with tattoos all over his hands, front and back. It must have been extremely painful getting tattooed on those parts of his body. He was selling Coca-Cola in vintage bottles; a very old design. They were actually still being made by a factory on the outskirts of Moscow. Each day he'd buy eight bottles from the factory for $7 - under a dollar per bottle. He'd then come to Novy Arbat and sell the bottles for $2 each. I bought a bottle from him. I got more drink in this $2 bottle than I did in the $6 cans of Coke in my Minibar at the Penta.

I was in Red Square again. The hot dog stand I saw the last time I was there had gone. A policeman with good English told me the story. A gang war had erupted over who got the protection money from the hot dog stand. Shooting began and in the mayhem the hot dog attendant was killed along with two mafia street men.

The problem was that everyone was earning a tiny wage of about $90 a month. If you succeeded, and people could see your success, you were done for. The hot dog stand was openly successful, taking in over $1,000 a day. People would literally kill for that kind of money.

With my money changed at a good rate, I went to the casino on Novy Arbat. Gordon, the Scottish manager, pulled me aside and said he'd been told not to allow Australians into the casino. It was a casino to casino tip-off from the Royal. I talked to Gordon for some time and persuaded him to let me play. The decision could have gone either way. I was getting thoroughly sick of Ponytail, Leon, and Sergei. Their behaviour was directly affecting my ability to make money and was putting me in danger, The others in my group were becoming a liability.

There weren't many people here to play poker tonight. If I hadn't been there the game wouldn't have started at all. Gordon was now happy that I was in his casino to play poker. The other players only had US dollars and needed to change their money to roubles. Since I'd changed $4,000 to roubles, and the poker game was smaller than the Royal's game, I was able to change money for the other poker players. I gave better rates than the casino was offering but worse rates than I'd got on the street when changing my own money. I made a good profit just on the currency transfers. Once the other poker players all had roubles, the game got underway.

I played for four hours, winning $2,000. I had also cleared $1,700 from the currency changing. This was big business. I was accumulating money at a great rate. About $15,000 in a week. The other people in my squad, the Australians or the immigrants as they were called, were failing and looking bad. The only thing going was the clothing shop which looked set to make a killing. Alex had taken over existing premises and was set to open any day now.

We all met at the office for a catch up. Sergei, as was always the case these days, was desperate for money and asked me how much I'd made last night. I told him that they won't let us into the Royal Casino anymore thanks to his visit with Ponytail and Leon. He refused to accept the blame, saying that the Royal was no good. I told him it was a great place for me to play and I gave him his 40% share of last night's $2,000, $800, in front of the others. He was amazed how much I was winning and the size of his cut. He demanded that I go and play blackjack in Gabriella's Casino with him, since he needed more money for everyone else's expenses.

Security at Gabriella's

So, Sergei took me to play blackjack at Gabriella's. This was my least favourite of the Moscow casinos but it was also the one least likely to kick us out. Luck was bad tonight, and I was down $2,000 after just fifteen minutes of play. Well, losses happen. At least Gabriella's wasn't gangster-only tonight. A big group of Chinese were playing at another table.

A Georgian mafia foot-soldier came over and asked me for $100. I told him I was losing $2,000 already, but if I won back my money I'd give him $100. He could see that I was losing and accepted my answer.

On another blackjack table, the Chinese were having a fantastic time. They had a few thousand dollars on the table and whenever the dealer busted, they gave out a loud cheer. They were all smiling, and they were having a lot of luck that night from the sound of things. They were going well for half an hour and when I looked over a third time, everyone had a big stack of chips in front of them. The Georgian gangster who'd approached me earlier was now watching the winning Chinese. After another dealer bust, he approached the Chinese, to ask them for $100. The Chinese told him to fuck off. The Georgian, not strong in English, asked a gangster friend what the Chinese guy had meant. A guy from a rival Russian gang piped up and said, "He wants to fuck you real good."

Really not the best way to calm down the situation. The other gangsters started laughing at the Georgian. He returned to the rest of his gang. They were simmering with anger. He went to the Chinese a second time and was given the same answer.

An hour later the Chinese guy who'd told the Georgian off needed a bathroom break. I saw as he was going into the men's bathroom that five Georgian gang members followed him in, like a pack of wolves. Two other gang members stood guard over the entrance and told anyone else approaching that this bathroom was closed and to use the other men's room right over there on that wall next to the cashier.

After a minute I heard screams from the guarded men's room. Then there were some sickening thuds, banging sounds like someone punching a wall, with more screaming. The manager looked at a few of the customers and then retreated to his office. Security also went outside, pretending that nothing was going on. A couple of the Chinese left their table to see what was happening. They were easily stopped by the Georgians guarding the bathroom entrance.

The attack lasted for ten minutes. Then the five assaulting gangsters simply walked out, with the two guards joining them. The bathroom was open for public use again.

A minute later the Chinese guy stumbled out of the bathroom. He was barely recognizable. He had three huge bumps on his head, and on one side of his face, teeth were missing. At least he could still walk, though in a strange limping way. The other Chinese rushed to his aid. While they did this, their blackjack table was unattended. Gangsters moved to that table and stole most of the chips from their stacks.

The Chinese approached the English manager for help. He was back on the floor now that the attack was over. He had seen nothing. The guy who'd been assaulted pointed at his neck, showing his jade necklace had been taken along with his Rolex watch. He'd had his trousers removed as well. At the back of his underwear were unmistakable blood stains. He said he'd been raped and from the visible evidence it seemed an honest complaint. So this is what can happen in a Russian casino. What a place!

The Chinese returned to their blackjack table and immediately noticed the theft of most of their chips. The dealer and the manager were no help to them. Players had to look after the security of their own chips. The casino's security now came onto the scene, and told the Chinese guy who'd been beaten and raped that he now had to leave, since he wasn't suitably dressed. The Chinese again appealed to the manager for help, but he smugly said that he couldn't do anything, other than go to the first aid box and get them some Band-Aids.

It was over for me at Gabriella's. I decided I wouldn't play there anymore. This was the toughest place on the planet. I'd lost $4,000 and needed to quit just from the money, let alone what I'd seen from the gangsters. One positive from this memorable experience was that when our casino finally opened, it would be very easy to attract the Chinese customers we would need. Word would spread around the Asians about what had happened at Gabriella's. None of them would go there anymore, it would then be our casino versus the Royal for the Chinese customers. Easy.

Disappearing Businessmen

Outside Gabriella's, we saw a big demonstration on the street. The communist old guard were protesting against President Boris Yeltsin. They were threatening to retake control. We were advised to keep our heads down; not speak English and stay off the streets for a while.

I returned to the casino on Novy Arbat. Gordon was happy to see me. He filled me in on the political unrest and the current protests. He introduced me to a Korean businessman, who was setting up an electronics store in the heart of Moscow.

The gangster groups at Novy Arbat tonight were all animated. It looked like something big had just gone down. My instincts were right. The top boss of one of the gangs, Otari Kvantrishvili, had just been assassinated. He rarely left his castle stronghold, and when he did, he had twenty security guards with him. But even those precautions hadn't been enough. A sniper had set up in the next building and had waited several days to get him. Otari was one of the most famous Mafia figures. His assassination was the talk of the town.

With the political protests, the streets were becoming dangerous for foreigners and immigrants. Despite this, or even because of it, the casinos were booming.

Back at the hotel, a message from Sergei told me to be at the office tomorrow for a meeting. I was happy to get some sleep. I'd seen some eye-opening things tonight, inside and outside the casinos. The already dangerous situation in Russia looked like it could spiral out of control at any moment.

At the office the next day, Sergei was in tears. He claimed that Otari had been a lifelong friend of his. He even told this to Wardrobe and some new outfit guys. He suggested we all go to Otari's funeral to pay our respects. Everyone in the Moscow underworld would be there.

I asked the meeting about the progress of our clothes-store guy, Alex, who had been absent from the last few meetings. Sayeed told me that all the merchandise was in the warehouse, ready to go, and the first shop was fully stocked, but nobody could tell me where Alex himself was. It sounded strange. Maybe he'd gone the way of the hot dog seller in Red Square.

I made another trip to Novy Arbat. This was easily my favourite place in all of Moscow. My expenses were ballpark $600 a day, and I was earning about $2,700 a day. The Korean guy offered me a share in his electronics business. I politely declined because I'd seen that most foreign-owned businesses in Moscow go under pretty quickly. There was too much hassle put on them once they showed any signs of success. There was the local government, the police, the gangsters, even the fire brigade, to be paid off.

The fire brigade paid a monthly visit to businesses and if they didn't pay a hefty "inspection fee" then the brigade would declare a defect with the premises and get the business shut down on the spot. It was yet another shakedown. The Korean boasted he could take care of all of this, he was well connected and had good protection.

I'd heard similar assurances from other foreign businessmen in Moscow before. They got involved with a group and they trusted that group to look after them. What they never saw was that the people protecting them were the very people they had to fear the most. This was the pattern in Moscow in 1993. Foreigners, sensing great opportunity, came to set up businesses, invest their money, train the staff, and share their skills. As soon as the businesses were operating and running smoothly, the mafia moved in and took over. The foreigners were run out of town.

Otari's Funeral

All of our gang went to Otari's funeral, in the ten black Mercedes. The other gangs and their leaders had even more people present. It was both a show of strength and a sign of respect.

The gang wars and enmities were put on hold for that day, though there was always a small chance that something would flare up. All-in-all there were over two thousand people at the funeral. It was an open casket, and after half an hour of the service, the church minister asked family and friends to have a last look at Otari before the burial. Twenty family and as many close friends lined up for their final viewing. The mother and wife kissed Otari's head, his face now at peace. Then to my amazement, Sergei joined the line. There were thirty other mafia bosses at the funeral but they didn't want to view the body and kiss Otari's head.

Sergei went to the coffin and started wailing. He then gently kissed the head of the deceased. He approached the wife and family and offered his condolences. What a shameful performance, I thought to myself. The other mobs must have thought Sergei was much more connected than he really was. Sergei wanted them to think he was well connected and on his way up in this world. Sayeed, the champion wrestler from Iran, was genuinely saddened by Otari's death. Otari was also a passionate wrestler and had set up clubs in Moscow and promoted the sport.

My New Apartment

I was going to be in Russia for another few months, so I went to look at a new apartment. I found an advertisement for one in Russia's English language newspaper, the Moscow Times. The Moscow Times was written by foreign journalists for other foreigners to enjoy. It had very entertaining stories of the crazy things that were going on in the city.

One story I'll never forget involved a middle-aged Russian hairdresser and a drug-addict who robbed her shop. The hairdresser caught him in the act and overpowered him. She then kept him for three days, feeding him nothing but black-market Viagra, and humped him five times a day. When she was arrested, she freely admitted to all of this but couldn't understand that she'd done anything wrong. After all it was the junkie who had tried to steal money and equipment from her salon. I'm not sure what Russian law she was charged under, but in Australia she was guilty. Australians involved in thieving can be charged as a "Receiver of Stolen Goods." The hairdresser was a "Receiver of Swollen Goods." Viagra-assisted swollen goods.

I went to see the advertised apartment. It was totally different to the hellhole that Sergei, Leon, Ponytail, and Sayeed were staying in. It had proper plumbing, modern fixtures, it was well worth the money they were asking for it. There was only one catch. It wasn't available for another two months, and the manager was demanding a $7,000 deposit to reserve it. It was the best place I'd seen, so I gave the manager my deposit, with a promise to move in after eight weeks.

Pleased with my day's work, I mentioned my apartment success to Gordon that night at the Novy Arbat. He burst out laughing.

"You put down a deposit on that new apartment on Vishneyka street, Joe?"

"Yeah, that's the place."

"You won't get to move in there. Nobody moves in there. Let me tell you about the scam."

The manager took money from foreigners as a deposit for his apartment. The apartment would be ready to move into in two months. If foreigners left Moscow or disappeared in those two months, too bad. Moscow was so volatile that 30% of people who paid their deposit never showed up two months later to move in. The manager kept all the forfeited deposits.

The 70% that did show up, Gordon explained, were fobbed off with a variety of excuses. The apartment was no longer available, someone else had taken it at a higher price, sorry nothing we can do but here is your $7,000 deposit back. I realised that I'd given $7,000 to a guy who had no intention of renting me an apartment and hoped that I wouldn't return to get my money back.

A week before my return date to the apartment, I came up with a plan. If the apartment owner was conning innocent foreigners, then he deserved the same treatment himself. I wasn't going to simply turn up on my own and listen to his bullshit stories and get my $7,000 back. I'd bring Sayeed and a few of his heavies. It would be interesting to hear this conman explain to them why the apartment was no longer available.

I turned up with Sayeed and his massive friends, and met the apartment manager. He had all the expected excuses about how I could no longer take the apartment and the best he could do was give me my deposit back. Then it came time for me to have my say.

"I think you can do better than that. You see, I've hired my friends here to help me move my furniture and my gear into the apartment. I've paid good money for their help and now they've got nothing to do and even after you give me my money back, I'll still be out of pocket. I suggest you give me $14,000 back. That will keep my friends happy."

Keeping my huge friends happy looked to be a very good idea indeed. The apartment manager reached into his safe, which had many other "deposits" in it, and gave me the $14,000 that I'd asked for. I gave some to Sayeed and his friends outside for their assistance in standing over the conman.

On the way back to the Penta it occurred to me that the apartment manager had been quick to resolve the situation and meet my demand for fourteen thousand. I should have taken him for twenty.

Our Casino Opens

I had three weeks to interview and hire staff for our casino. With the problems I was having with our mafia, I did my job half-heartedly. I just went through the motions and did the bare minimum I could to get by. I would do what I promised to do to get a room running, but there was nothing in it for me and I was already starting to think of escape and my next move, if only I could get out of Moscow.

The gang wanted the dealers and hospitality staff to all be women, the prettier the better. I wanted competent staff. From the first round of interviews, I had five men and forty-five women, making a long list of fifty. We needed twenty staff for the opening week. The gang encouraged me to get rid of all the men on the list but there was one fantastic young man, Ivan, who was superbly presented and had excellent English. I couldn't let him go. I would give Ivan a job in a London casino, he was that good. The final group of twenty was him with nineteen ladies. I used Ivan to help train the other staff members.

The mafia made me fire him. I had a long interview with him and passed him some cash with my full apologies. He wouldn't take the cash. The next day he turned up for work as though nothing had happened. I loved his audacity. We opened with that staff of twenty and in our first month we were helped by the protests in the streets and the danger of an uprising. The government imposed a curfew. People couldn't be seen outside after 7 p.m. and before 6 a.m. This actually helped our poker and casino games. Players got to the casino before 7 p.m., played overnight, relaxed in the bar for an hour and staggered out into the morning. The curfew was great for the casino and the players enjoyed it too. We had an overnight captive audience.

Exit Plan

As I feared, Alex was gone. Missing presumed dead. Our mob had taken over his stores. They planned to sell all the stock but not pay the staff or the rent. Make a quick killing. On top of the quick killing they had already made. In their mind it was better to make a million in a month and fly by night instead of a hundred thousand a month for the next five years.

The Korean electronics expert escaped with his life but nothing else. His store was stocked with about five million dollars' worth of gear. One Monday morning, he came in to find half of his stock gone and his two security guards drunk and asleep on the floor. The mob the Korean was working with, who he paid for protection and security, washed their hands of the affair and were probably behind the theft themselves. He reported the theft to the police who were unsympathetic and asked to see receipts to prove he'd paid import duties on his electronics. The police took the Korean into the store's corner office, pulled down the blinds and stood over him while he went through his accounts and receipts. Other police waited outside on the shop floor. Five hours later, when they finally let the Korean out of his own office, the rest of his stock had gone. The police chief was insulted by the suggestion that the second theft could have been the act of his upstanding policemen. He told the Korean that he should leave the country. Russia was not his kind of place. Moscow in 1993 must have been the most dangerous city in the world.

I considered my options. Investing in any business was crazy. You ended up robbed or killed, probably both. Casino management was no safer. Half of the managers so far had been killed and most of the others had taken savage beatings. Now that the casino was running, my ongoing value to the Russians was limited. Once they thought they could handle things themselves, I'd be moved on. At best I'd be bashed and robbed, and I'd escape from Russia a broken man. If they thought I knew too much, then I wouldn't make it out of here alive. I had to get out. Ponytail and Sayeed were also looking for their own ways out.

My exit visa was in Leon's safe. Leon was controlling us, keeping us in Moscow and forcing us to work for them. The profit share we'd been promised in the first meetings was gone. We were expected to run the casino for the mob and then further down the track, we'd be dealt with.

The next time I went to the office, I saw the bizarre sight of Sayeed handcuffed to a bathroom sink for a day. He was beaten until he swore that he would co-operate. Sayeed had asked for his exit visa back and this was their answer. If he didn't soften after this beating, he'd be put in the basement prison for a few days. I had to play along with this bullying.

I faced two problems. The first was how to get my exit visa back and the second was how to bring my cash out of the country and make my escape. One of my friends in the foreign business community was a Londoner named Frank King. On top of his business interests, he said he was a professional poker player. Like many businessmen in Moscow, he was being screwed over and was planning his own escape from Russia. He suggested that I get a new exit visa from the Australian embassy.

"Go to the embassy, Joe. It's the only way. You'll have to tell them your story, how your exit visa was taken from you. They can get you a new one. Then we can get out of here." He made a lot of sense. I did as he suggested, and the embassy helped me out. I had to sit through an interview with the Russian police, who I suspected were on the take. Word would get back to my mafia at lightning speed that I was planning to jump.

Airport Escape

Frank and I booked the same flight - Moscow to Rome. I went to the Australian embassy to pick up my new documents. A high-ranking diplomat sat me down for a final talking-to.

"Two of my staff are going to the airport with you this afternoon, Joe."

"Thanks for the offer, but I can handle this myself. I know how to get on a plane."

"And there are people who know how to stop you getting on a plane. I want you to get safely to Rome. Let's make sure that happens."

He wouldn't take no for an answer. Three hours later, two embassy staff and I were at the airport. There were about a dozen gangsters at the airport, alone and in pairs. I didn't know their faces, but I could see what they were. My escorts stayed with me right through to the departure lounge. Frank King was there waiting for the flight.

An old Russian man motioned to me. Come here, come here, I've got something for you, his gestures suggested. I moved towards him but one of my escorts pulled me back. Whatever this stranger wanted, it wouldn't turn out well. I got safely on the plane and sat next to Frank. In the air, I looked out of the window for a birds-eye view of this beautiful city. I'd escaped by the skin of my teeth from another dangerous situation, but I felt in my heart that I hadn't seen the last of Moscow.

Three Capitals

Frank and I talked poker and gambling all the way to Rome. I'd managed to get most of my money out of Moscow. A lot of it was in Swiss francs and German deutschmarks. Poker professional Frank said we had to go to the United States and take on the casinos there. He knew blackjack card counting and we could work as a team to make some easy money doing that. We'd also make a lot of money with our poker skills. I liked this plan.

In Rome, we arranged for travel visas to the United States. It would take five days for them to come through. The visas would allow us to stay in the United States for a full year. We booked flights to Los Angeles.

With a five day wait for our visas, Frank needed some action. He suggested we play poker heads-up. He warned me to expect no mercy. We were playing for keeps. I wouldn't be able to beg him for my money back.

By the time our visas were ready, it was Frank doing the begging. He'd lost all of his money to me. For a poker professional, he was a bad player. If Frank could win big in the States, then it would be easy pickings for me.

We left Rome for the United States. Frank had good USA knowledge and knew where to stay and the place to go. We expected to stay in the States for the full year, then return to Rome, but our plans were flexible.

It took just over a week to get from Moscow to Rome to Los Angeles. As our flight approached the west coast of the United States, I felt happy with what I'd achieved and excited by what lay ahead. I'd proven myself as a gambler in Australia and done as well as I could in Moscow. Gangs could double-cross me and stiff me over, but in a fair fight I knew I could come out on top. Two days later we left Los Angeles on a short domestic flight.

I had the money. I had the desire. I had a year in this town, make or break. I was in my third capital in ten days. Moscow was the capital of the eastern world and Rome was the capital of the ancient world. I was now in the capital of the gambling world. I was in Las Vegas.

Coming Soon: Part Two

Joe Cammarano has successfully left Russia and enjoys a great year in Las Vegas. He wins in poker games of all kinds at high stakes. But the biggest games are now in Europe. Chasing the big money, the man from Australia goes to Austria. The games are big in Vienna but they are also crooked. Criminal teams are working on the poker tables to cheat the unwary. Joe must find a new way to win.

A new Russian opportunity arises, and Joe returns to Moscow. He gains the trust and protection of Russia's biggest gambler. Joe's success causes envy and resentment. As the Russians plot to bring him down, he faces his biggest challenge yet. Can he succeed in the toughest place on Earth?

Joe Cammarano Will Return

www.ingramcontent.com/pod-product-compliance
Lightning Source LLC
LaVergne TN
LVHW091553060526
838200LV00036B/812